BACON
THE COOKBOOK
Niamh Shields

Cover Illustration, Interior Design and Layout Tim Biddle
Editors Karyn Noble, Anne Pichon
Photographer Georgia Glynn Smith, excluding photos on pages 26-27, 44-45, 54, 62-63, 65, 66-67, 72-73, 110-111, 113, 114-115, 123, 147
Art Direction and Design for Photography Anita Mangan

First published in 2020 by Niamh Shields, Eat Like a Girl
eatlikeagirl.com

Second Edition published 2021

ISBN: 978-1-8383155-1-1

Printed in Italy

Bacon: The Cookbook!

Introduction

Bacon Brunch

Bacon Bites

Feel-Good Comfort Food

Feeding Friends

Bacon BBQ

Bacon is Sweet

Bacon Pantry

Bacon Curing

- Maple bacon
- Hot toddy bacon
- Miso maple bacon
- Stout and treacle bacon
- Seaweed bacon
- Gochujang, soy and lime bacon

Small Baconpedia

Your Bacon Space

Index

Acknowledgements

Bacon: The Cookbook!

Hello! And welcome to my wonderful world of bacon. I am so happy that you are here.
After many years of having all of this circle in my head, it is a huge pleasure to share it with you.

If a book is a portal to another world, and even a cookbook can be this, maybe even especially
a cookbook at times, this is a portal to a magical bacon place. This is not the first bacon book and
it won't be the last, but it is one that celebrates all of bacon's virtues: savoury and especially sweet.

Bacon stands apart for many reasons, not least of which, it is at once one of the most
overestimated ingredients, but it is also one of the most underestimated. This book recognises the
strengths of bacon and not just in its saltiness and umami depth, but also its gentle sweetness and
its versatility. That sees just how well it plays with others and sets up those play dates. That allows
bacon to play repeatedly with favourite friends (you will notice some ingredients pop up regularly
enough).

I am a woman of many passions, food and cooking being central to my existence. I love it and it
makes me so very happy. I spend much of my day in my London kitchen, wooden spoon in hand,
crafting recipes and tasty things to eat. Unless I'm travelling and finding new things to eat, like
crocodile bacon at a food market in the Borneo jungle (or right next to it, at least!). Crocodile
bacon? I am glad I tried it but I will stick with the original.

That of course was pre-pandemic, which is where we are now. It seems a good time to be in the
kitchen creating good things to eat and a good time to share a book with you that is packed with
difference and interesting concepts to brighten these long evenings.

Where did this bacon obsession come from?

My bacon obsession started with a taste of bacon jam, and I haven't looked back since.
My excitable palate has powered me fiercely ahead, exploring the myriad possibilities.
Bacon is a great culinary conversationalist. I was quickly hooked. Not long after, I started
hosting and teaching Bacon Masterclasses and my Sunday Bacon Club: both fun and slightly
outrageous cooking classes centred around bacon.

Then I took the bacon show on the road. I did a Bacon Masterclass on stage at Electric Picnic
in Ireland and I brought Sunday Bacon Club to Wilderness Festival in the UK and taught lots of
people how to rescue their hangovers with bacon buttermilk waffles while they made candied
bacon, bacon jam, candied bacon fudge and flapjacks. That all set me on a bacon track, which
arrived eventually at this book and these recipes.

Bacon and Ireland

In Ireland (where I am from) and in many other countries, many parts of the pig were traditionally cured as bacon to preserve the meat throughout the year. It is more common to eat regular back bacon and streaky bacon now, not as sustenance but as a bit of excitement on the plate. Bacon chops and ribs are available in many butchers still, though. It is a normal thing.

There are nods throughout the book to the unofficial Irish national dish, boiled bacon and cabbage. We are not the only country to combine the two (China and Japan do it brilliantly) but it is a source of much comfort for most Irish people. Yes, we love Irish stew, but that is more for an occasion. Bacon and cabbage is the dish that your mother made for you at home occasionally. Simple and lovely. Perfect when the bacon is sliced and served with parsley sauce if it is the weekend.

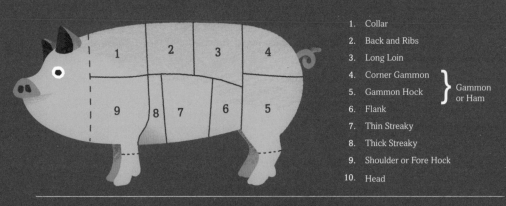

1. Collar
2. Back and Ribs
3. Long Loin
4. Corner Gammon ⎫
5. Gammon Hock ⎬ Gammon or Ham
6. Flank   ⎭
7. Thin Streaky
8. Thick Streaky
9. Shoulder or Fore Hock
10. Head

Methods of cooking

Collar: may be boiled, or sliced and fried.

Back: ⎫
Long Loin: ⎭ Expensive part. Usually cut for rashers.

Corner Gammon: ⎫
Gammon Ham: ⎭ May be boiled or baked, sometimes boned.

Flank: Economical part - used for boiling.

Thin Streaky: May be cut for rashers, or used for boiling.

Thick Streaky: Cut for rashers or used for boiling.

Shoulder: Used for boiling, sometimes boned.

Porksteak: Removed from loin before curing, and sold fresh.

Head: Used for boiling

Based on P53 from "All in the Cooking, Colaiste Mhuire Book of Advanced Cookery" (by Josephine B. Marnell, Nora M. Breathnach, Ann A. Martin and Mor Murnaghan). See p.214 for details and the original page.

Evolution of Bacon: the Cookbook

This book has been a long time coming and has been through several iterations over the years. It is a much better book for that. With each evolution of the book itself and the recipes within, I realised that I wanted to simplify it, and that made this book better. Simplicity is much harder than the alternative. You have to be very confident in what you are sharing, and that is something that is earned through intimately getting to know and tweaking every recipe in the book. That takes time.

I started wanting to make a definitive bacon book but realised that it is the task of a lifetime. So, I shifted the focus. This book is intended as a relaxed guide and a friend in the kitchen for the home cook who wants to push the boundaries and try something new and exciting. It is intended as a joyful ode to the flavour possibilities and potential of bacon for the home kitchen, with lots of recipes to guide you through.

You can put bacon in everything, but should you? That is entirely up to you. I am here to show you the scope of bacon and encourage you to try new things. Ultimately when this book is yours, it is your own. A recipe is a guide and every recipe is yours to tweak to your taste (with the exception of the confectionery and sweet baking recipes which have to be precise to work).

The recipes in this book

When I started this book I was obsessed with bacon everywhere all the time. Everything from scratch. Bacon from scratch. Bacon stock only! As time progressed I realised that this book would serve a better purpose if it was more pragmatic and useful. I didn't want to write a book that would mainly look pretty on a shelf. Eventually, I came back to my core culinary values: eat well, as best as you can in that moment, and with what you have.

I will always aim to produce recipes that get the best results with minimal effort. If there is a lot of effort, it is because it is essential (I am looking at you Candied Bacon Fudge). Every recipe needs to stand on its own and make absolute sense. The hope is that this book shows you a new way of looking at and experiencing something that is familiar.

I decided to avoid the bacon clichés, the bacon lattices, the bacon explosion, the bacon taco bowls. I did try some of them. A bacon explosion that actually exploded and leaked molten cheese all over my BBQ. I will leave those ideas to others, as they are not my style.I focused instead on ideas that were more in line with my view of the world through bacon goggles.

Bacon has favourite friends. Sugar, chocolate, maple syrup and bacon love each other. Bacon loves a bit of booze. Whiskey, rum, bourbon, vodka, cider. Bacon loves some vinegar to balance its sweet salty self out. Bacon itself is naturally sweet, salty and has deep umami flavour. Bacon fat brings so much flavour.

You will see some repeating patterns and references. Many of these things are favourites of mine, which of course helps, but they are here because they are friends of bacon and I am but a witness. Some things are just too good not to repeat.

Curing your own bacon

You'll find plenty of curing recipes and a detailed but accessible explainer of how to cure your own bacon at home. I talk about nitrites, but it is opt-in and in its own section. Not all of you will want to cure your own bacon, and you don't need to, but if I could encourage you to cure just one thing, cure your own bacon chops and make them with maple syrup. They will be ready in a few days. Of course, you can buy bacon too, I do. There is no judgement in this book or any purism when it comes to curing your own. This book is intended for pleasure and enjoyment, a culinary adventure.

A whistle-stop recipe tour from brunch to sweets

The book is broken down as I like to eat and in the ways that I love to cook bacon. So, beginning with Brunch because, well, brunch is key. Then Bacon Bites to have with friends or in front of the TV or with a book on a stolen afternoon. Some snacks the size of your hand, some smaller, all gorgeous. On then to Feel-Good Comfort Food because isn't that the truth? There's a chapter of some classics with my take, and some inventions of my own from my hungry belly and head to your kitchen. Don't delve into that phrase too much. There are recipes for roasting bacon, for bacon chops and for bacon ribs. Bacon isn't just about frying a streaky slice until crisp, although I will never ever knock that. It is so much more though, and I wanted to take it further.

Bacon recipes for feeding friends and brightening your home BBQ

Where do we go from there? We feed friends! These recipes are really all about the weekends when you have time, but none of these will keep you from your friends for too long or trap you unnecessarily next to a pot with enormous FOMO and developing despair on what should be a happy moment. Yes, the beer cheese dip requires your presence, but it is brief and the rewards are enormous. It is followed by Bacon BBQ and really there is much flexibility between these two chapters. You can cook these things in the oven or on the hob/stovetop if the BBQ doesn't appeal. If you love a BBQ, you will love these bacon recipes for it. Please cook the ribs.

Bacon is sweet

Bacon is underestimated in its versatility. It is fantastic in sweet recipes, and that is why the sweet chapter is one of the longest and one of my favourites. The candied bacon fudge takes time and attention but it deserves both in spades. It is old-school with a new twist. Once you have mastered this fudge, and if you drink whiskey – spelled the Irish way, of course – or bourbon, you must have it with a glass. It is a perfect match.

And now, over to you!

This book was a long time in the making and I want to thank all who have supported it from the beginning and even before. Every backer, everyone who offered advice, especially if I didn't want to hear it. There were many bends in the road, and many hurdles, but, very happily, here we are now. This would never have happened without you.

It makes me so happy to know that you are reading it, and that it is in your hands, and in your kitchen. That makes me happier than you will ever know and I wish you many happy hours cooking.

Bacon the Cookbook started with me, and now it is yours

Bacon the Cookbook finishes with some pages for you: pages where you can write your own bacon recipes, or add ones that I will continue to share. These are your notes pages, your very own bacon scratchings with your own pen.

I will be sharing new bacon recipes via baconthecookbook.com (and on the respective social media channels: @baconthecookbook on Instagram and Facebook) that you can also add to these pages. There is a newsletter on baconthecookbook.com that you can sign up for too.

Some final advice

Before we start, a piece of advice for the bacon-curious. Candied bacon is something you must always make extra of, as there is never enough. Bacon jam, even more so, and you will likely eat it all. It is too good. Always make extra, it is the ultimate condiment.

Let's get started!

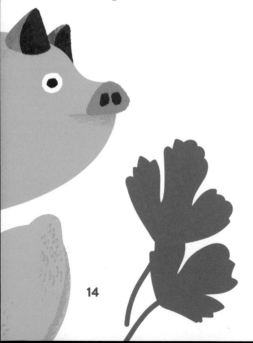

Bacon Brunch

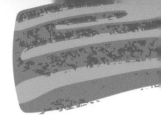

Bacon Brunch

Brunch is the one, isn't it? It just is. Brunch is breakfast with attitude at a more appropriate time. Who likes eating first thing? I eat breakfast because it is good for me, I eat brunch because I really want to.

If you need persuading, and I doubt you do as you are here reading this, humour me.

You can have brunch anytime (really you can, don't trust anyone who says otherwise).

Brunch often features bacon, and when you make your own brunch, you can make sure it always does! Shout out to eggs too, bacon's best friend along with bourbon and maple syrup. They make a tasty crew.

You can make it boozy (and bring bacon in here too with my Bacon Bloody Mary).

You can do brunch solo with the weekend's newspapers and a huge pot of coffee (that's me!) or you can be social and have a big brunch gathering with friends (that's me too).

Brunch is big and satisfying. Brunch is a meal that grabs you by the chops and sits you down and tells you that everything is going to be ok. So, get the coffee on (ok, tea is also acceptable) and let's get cooking!

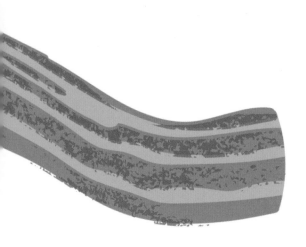

Cheesy bacon French toastie

INGREDIENTS

Makes: 1 toastie (multiply ingredients for servings as appropriate)

enough slices of bacon to cover the bread generously, about 4

butter, enough for buttering the bread and frying the toastie

2 slices of bread

1 slice of good cheese to cover the bacon *(I like Cheddar here, but choose your favourite)*

2 eggs

a splash of milk

I still remember when I first had French toast or what we used to call 'eggy bread', and what a revelation it was. It is still a morning favourite and reaches another level of pleasure when bacon and cheese are introduced to the mix. For this, a smaller-size bread is easier to manage, both in terms of cooking and indeed eating, as it is quite rich.

METHOD

1. Fry the bacon. When cooked to your liking, remove it from the pan to a plate and set aside. Save the bacon fat for another use (you must have a bacon drippings jar. Liquid gold!).

2. Make your sandwich. Butter the bread and place the bacon on the buttered side of one slice. Put the cheese on top of the bacon and place the other slice of bread on top, buttered side down. Press down well so that it holds together.

3. Beat the eggs and milk in a shallow, large bowl (large enough to fit the sandwich comfortably) and dip the sandwich in, ensuring it is well covered on both sides.

4. Put a knob of butter in a frying pan that is big enough to accommodate the sandwich and heat over a medium heat. Convert your lovely sandwich to a toastie by frying it gently on both sides until golden brown. Eat immediately.

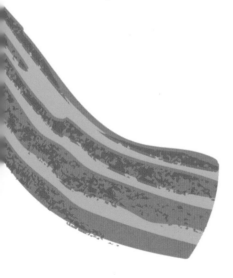

Maple bacon granola

INGREDIENTS

Serves: 4

75g *(2¾ oz)* blanched
    almonds

50g *(1¾ oz)* pumpkin
    seeds

250g *(9 oz)* porridge oats
    *(I like to use the larger
    jumbo size)*

50g *(1¾ oz)* butter

50ml *(2 fl oz)* maple
    syrup

100g *(3½ oz)* maple
    candied bacon, diced
    (see p.198)

2 sharp apples, such as
    Granny Smith, cores
    and stems removed,
    cut into small dice

To serve:

yoghurt

maple syrup

This granola is a gorgeous tumble of sweet, bright and deep, crisp bacon loveliness. It comes together quickly, and candied small bites of bacon bring a cheeky pop to the bowl. Make a lot or make a little. It makes a perfect start to a weekend brunch and a good speedy weekday breakfast.

METHOD

1. In a dry frying pan, toast the almonds and pumpkin seeds over a medium-high heat until the pumpkin seeds start to pop and the almonds brown a little. Stir as you do, and take care not to burn them (they both have a lot of oil and so can burn if left unattended).

2. As soon as the pumpkin seeds start to pop add the oats, and toast for a further minute until golden. Remove from the pan to a cool plate or bowl and leave to the side.

3. Melt the butter in the same pan, add the maple syrup and allow the butter and syrup to cook for a few minutes over a medium heat, allowing the maple syrup to approach caramelisation and the butter to brown, but not burn. So, you need to watch this. When it smells like caramel and has thickened a bit it is ready!

4. Add the candied bacon, apples, oats, seeds and nuts, and stir until well coated. At this point, you can store this granola in a sealed container in the fridge for up to a week until you want to use it.

5. To serve, add a dollop of yoghurt. And a little extra drizzle of maple syrup never hurt anyone, now did it?

Maple bacon rolls

INGREDIENTS

For the bacon and maple filling:

100ml *(3½ fl oz)* maple syrup

16 slices streaky bacon

For the bread dough:

550g *(1lb 3½ oz)* strong white flour *(bread flour)*

50g *(1¾ oz)* golden caster sugar

1 tsp salt

7g *(¼ oz)* fast-action dried yeast

250ml whole milk *(8½ fl oz)*

1 large egg

100g *(3½ oz)* butter

For the cream cheese frosting:

50g *(1¾ oz)* cream cheese

4 tbsp maple syrup

2 tbsp bourbon

These are an essential for brunch with friends (as with my Bacon Sausage Bread, p.44). You can also win over difficult people with these, I assure you. These Maple Bacon Rolls are a bacon spin on everyone's favourite, cinnamon rolls. Borrowing only the shape and the idea of a frosting, everything else is completely different. The bacon has a bath in maple syrup while you make the bread, soaking up that gorgeousness and sweetness.

For a very tasty alternative, use bacon jam (see p.202) as a filling (with no extra maple syrup). Or bacon jam and cheese! Endless delicious possibilities.

METHOD

1. Prepare your bacon and maple filling by combining the maple syrup and the bacon in a bowl and massaging it well. Cover and leave in the fridge to marinade until the bread dough is ready.

2. Prepare the dough, either with a dough hook or by hand.

USING A MIXER WITH DOUGH HOOK: Bread is always easiest in a mixer with a dough hook. If using one, simply put all the bread dough ingredients in the mixing bowl, and with the dough hook combine everything at the slowest speed (so that the flour doesn't go everywhere!) and let it mix until the dough has lost its rough texture and acquired some elasticity, which you can test by stretching it (this takes about 5–6 minutes usually). As an enriched dough, it is naturally soft, but if it feels sticky, add flour a tablespoon at a time. One will likely be enough.

BY HAND: If you are doing this by hand, it doesn't take much longer than the dough-hook method. Combine the dry bread dough ingredients and mix in a big mixing bowl (or on a big board, if you have one) and set aside. In a separate bowl, mix the milk and egg, then melt the butter and add it to the wet ingredients. Slowly add the wet ingredients to the dry ingredients, mixing as you do. As an enriched dough, it is naturally soft, but if it feels sticky, add flour a tablespoon at a time. One will likely be enough. Knead with gusto for approximately 10 minutes until the dough has lost its rough texture and acquired some elasticity (which you can test by stretching it).

3. Cover the bowl with a dry, clean tea towel and allow your dough to rest in the warmest part of your kitchen or in the airing cupboard untilit is double in size. This will usually take an hour to an hour and a half.

4. Punch the dough to knock the air out, and let it settle for 5 minutes.

5. Remove the dough from the bowl and roll it into a sausage shape on a lightly floured board. Divide the dough into half with a knife, divide each half again, and then one more time, which will leave you with eight equal portions.

6. Retrieve the bacon and maple syrup from the fridge. Roll each dough segment into a long sausage shape that is about 1 inch/2.5cm in diameter. Flatten slightly, place 2 slices of maple-infused bacon on top and roll into a coil or snail shape. You can arrange them on a floured baking tray as individual rolls, or in a circle next to each other to make a tear-and-share version by placing one in the middle and arranging the others around it. This works best in a round dish with sides.

7. Preheat your oven to 200°C/180°Fan (400°F). Allow the rolls to sit at room temperature while you wait, to prove further. Bake for 18–20 minutes until golden.

8. While the rolls are baking, whisk all the cream cheese frosting ingredients together. Drizzle the frosting on top of the rolls when they are done and serve. Gorgeous hot but also good cold.

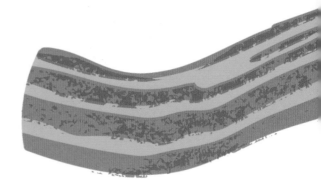

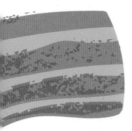

Eggs with bacon & cheese dippers

INGREDIENTS

Serves: 1

enough sliced bacon to cover 1 slice of bread in a single layer

enough butter for spreading bread

2 slices of bread of your choice

enough grated cheese to cover *(I suggest a combination of Parmesan and Gruyère or a good Cheddar)*

1 or 2 eggs, at room temperature, cooked any way you wish *(but best to keep a runny yolk)*

Tiny ham-and-cheese toasties to dip in your perfect yolk. Simple and lovely. An absolute treat. A runny egg yolk is an instant sauce, and this little twist makes your brunch eggs even better.

Boil your eggs, fry or poach them. Just make sure that your egg yolk is molten and dippy! My method is to add the eggs carefully to a pot of boiling water and time them for 5–6 minutes, depending on just how runny you like it. It is very important that they are at room temperature, for cooking generally, and particularly here to prevent temperature shock and the egg cracking.

Precision of measurements makes no sense here, as it all depends on the size of your bread of choice. Go with your heart.

METHOD

1. Fry your bacon in a frying pan and save the rendered fat. Always save the fat!

2. Combine some butter with the rendered bacon fat and spread this mixture on the outside of the two slices of bread that will make the sandwich: the bit that will hit the pan. Buttering the outside of the bread before frying it ensures that it goes a lovely crisp golden brown and it also enhances the flavour.

3. Putting the bacon-buttered side down, place your cooked bacon on one slice of the bread. Then add the cheese. I know you will be tempted to go wild here as you put your sandwich together, but don't. You need to be able to cut the sandwich into soldiers (strips), so go easy unless you want to torch your fingers as you eat. Put the second slice of bread on top, buttered side facing out.

4. Put the sandwich in a solid frying pan (cast iron works really well, but use whatever you have) over a medium heat. If you have a bacon press (an appliance that's usually cast iron with a handle, used regularly to press bacon so that it goes nice and crisp) put this on top of the sandwich. If you don't, put a slice of greaseproof paper on top and weigh it down with something heavy, like a tin of tomatoes or beans (or two!).

5. As the sandwich is frying, cook your egg(s) to personal preference (see above).

6. When the sandwich is golden and crisp at the bottom (you will smell it), carefully turn it (best to use tongs, as it will be hot) and continue to fry it until it is cooked on the other side.

7. Slice your toasted sandwich into soldiers (about two fingers wide) and dip into your waiting gorgeous egg(s).

Bacon ricotta pancakes with apple and sage

INGREDIENTS

Makes: approx. 8 pancakes

For the pancake batter:

200g *(7 oz)* ricotta cheese

100ml *(3½ fl oz)* milk

2 eggs

75g *(2¼ oz)* plain flour

1 tsp baking powder

pinch of sea salt

For the sage garnish:

10 sage leaves

butter, for frying

For the apple mixture:

25g *(1 oz)* butter

2 tbsp maple syrup, plus extra to serve

2 apples *(I like Gala or Discovery; use ones that are not overly sweet but also have some sharpness),* peeled, cored and cut into wedges

extra butter, for pancake frying

1 slice of bacon to serve per pancake *(but obviously as much as you like!)*

These fluffy bacon and ricotta pancakes are a more delicate approach to brunch. Fluffy American-style pancakes meets cheesecake meets bacon, apple and sage.

These pancakes are luxurious but they are also light. The ricotta gives them a pillowy yet creamy feel, the apples infuse a lovely sweetness that bounces off the bacon, and the sage a layer of savoury crispness. Fried sage is an absolute gem of an ingredient and a perfect garnish.

As with all pancakes, these are best if the batter is allowed to sit for a bit before frying. Let it rest for an hour to allow glutens to stretch. The starch molecules swell also, which means the mixture will get a little thicker, the end result being a pancake with a lighter texture.

METHOD

1. Make your pancake batter first. Mix the ricotta, milk and eggs and combine well with a fork or whisk in a mixing bowl.

2. Sift the flour and baking powder into the mixing bowl and add a pinch of salt. (Sifting introduces air and lightness.) Stir the flour in gently.

3. Fry off a small portion of the batter and taste to check seasoning; adjust the remaining batter if necessary, then rest the batter for an hour in the fridge.

4. While the batter is resting, prepare the other ingredients. Fry the sage leaves in a little melted butter until crisp (taking care to remove them gently before they go dark brown). Drain on kitchen paper and set aside.

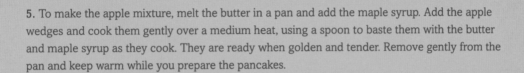

5. To make the apple mixture, melt the butter in a pan and add the maple syrup. Add the apple wedges and cook them gently over a medium heat, using a spoon to baste them with the butter and maple syrup as they cook. They are ready when golden and tender. Remove gently from the pan and keep warm while you prepare the pancakes.

6. You can fry three pancakes at a time in a large frying pan. Add some butter to the pan and when melted add approximately half a ladleful of batter per pancake to the pan. Cook gently over a medium heat. When holes start to bubble through the surface, they are ready to flip. Flip and cook on the remaining side until golden, which should just take a couple of minutes.

7. While the pancakes are cooking, fry the bacon to desired crispness.

8. Serve immediately or keep the pancakes warm in a low oven while you fry the remaining ones (and you could keep the apples in the oven too). Serve the pancakes in small stacks with apple wedges and bacon on top and an extra drizzle of maple syrup. Place the crisp sage leaves on top, taking care as they break very easily. They are worth it, though, as they taste great.

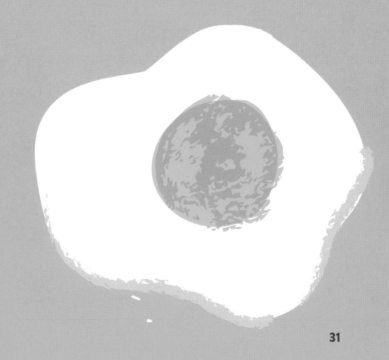

Bacon & egg cups

INGREDIENTS

Ingredients per cup

Makes: 12 (if using 12-cup baking tray)

Ingredients per cup of baking tray *(multiply by 12 for a 12-cup tray, for example):*

butter or oil, for greasing the tray

enough streaky bacon to line each tray cup with bacon, so that there are no gaps, approx. 3 slices per cup *(see note above)*

baking beans *(or any dried beans)*

1 thick slice tomato

fresh thyme leaves *(a small pinch removed from the stem for each cup)*

1 medium egg

1 tbsp single/pouring cream

1 tsp finely grated Parmesan cheese

These are simple and lovely and ideal for a social brunch. Kids love them, especially. You can make bigger ones in muffin trays, or small ones in bun trays (I like to use quail eggs for these if I am feeling fancy, and more importantly, patient).

In terms of bacon, you need enough to line the trays so that each hole of your tray has a bacon-shaped cup with no gaps. It will depend on the size of the tray cups, and on the size of your bacon but 2 slices of streaky bacon should do it. If you have leftovers, more to serve with it! Nothing lost, only bacon gained.

Use smaller-sized eggs for these: medium will be fine. Or if, like me, you are feeling fancy and have the dexterity and patience to manage quail eggs, go ahead and do it.

METHOD

1. Preheat your oven to 180°C/160°Fan (350°F).

2. Grease your baking tray with some butter (a butter wrapper is ideal) or brush some oil on.

3. Line each cup in the baking tray with the sliced bacon, taking care that there are no gaps, but also so that each cup holds a single layer of bacon with room for the filling.

4. Put a little square of greaseproof paper (big enough to cover the bacon) on each and fill with baking beans (you can just use dried beans and then save them to reuse another time). Bake for 10 minutes.

5. Remove the tray from the oven and remove the squares of greaseproof paper and the beans, taking care as the beans will be hot. Store the beans for a future use when making this again, or blind-baking pastry.

6. Into each tray cup put a slice of tomato, the pinch of thyme leaves, an egg (it is easier if you crack it into a ramekin or small bowl first) and finish with the cream (pour it gently over the yolk to protect it) and the Parmesan.

7. Repeat as you need to for each tray cup. Cover the tray with foil and put back in the oven for 10 minutes or until the eggs are done to your liking.

8. Remove from the oven and remove the bacon and egg cups gently from the tray. Serve immediately.

Cheesy potato waffles with bacon & kale

INGREDIENTS

Makes: approx. 2 waffles

25g *(1 oz)* plain flour

½ tsp bicarbonate of soda

25g *(1 oz)* butter

250g *(9 oz)* mashed
   floury potatoes *(like
   Maris Piper or Russet)* –
   approx. 325g *(11½ oz)*
   raw weight,
   when peeled

1 clove garlic, peeled and
   finely chopped

50g *(1¾ oz)* finely
   chopped, cooked bacon

3 spring onions,
   ends removed
   and finely sliced

25g *(1 oz)* finely
   grated Cheddar

1 egg

50ml *(2fl oz)* milk

sea salt, to taste

75g *(2¼ oz)* kale

olive oil, for sautéing kale

extra butter, for brushing
   on your waffle maker

To serve *(optional):*
eggs, cooked to
   your liking

Call me an Irish cliché (do! I embrace it!), but I adore the humble spud. They are a near perfect food. Soothing; nutritious; flexible; varied in texture, colour and taste; and they play so well with other flavours. Crisp them, mash them, turn them into gnocchi, pancakes or bread. Better yet? Make homemade potato waffles. So good.

Homemade potato waffles are different from the supermarket variety. A distant relative, maybe. They are more potato packed, and you can add butter and cheese and other wonderful things. It is a perfect use for leftover mashed potato. I prefer to make these with a floury potato, so Maris Piper or Russet would be good choices here.

To get good dry mash, if you are preparing some for these, I like to bake potatoes while I am using the oven for something else. Baked potatoes are drier than boiled or steamed and make great mash. The best mash for me is made using a potato ricer. This technique (baked potato and ricer) is excellent for gnocchi too. So, if you like both potato waffles and gnocchi, a potato ricer is a worthwhile investment.

METHOD

1. Mix the flour with the bicarbonate of soda, ensuring no lumps. Mash the butter into the potatoes, then add the mixed flour and bicarbonate of soda, garlic, bacon, spring onions and Cheddar.

2. Separately beat the egg with the milk, and add to the potato mix slowly, mixing gently as you do. Season with a generous pinch of sea salt and fry off a small bit to check the seasoning.

3. Prepare your kale by sautéing in some olive oil and sea salt until just softened, which should take just a few minutes.

4. Preheat your waffle maker. Brush the waffle plates with some butter and place half the potato mix on each waffle plate (for regular rectangular waffles). Cook until golden brown outside. Serve immediately with the kale and eggs of your choice.

Stove-top eggs in bacon and tomato sauce

INGREDIENTS

Serves: 1

50g *(1¾ oz)* streaky bacon *(I like streaky here, as the fat imparts extra flavour to the sauce)*, sliced into strips

1 tbsp neutral oil *(such as sunflower oil)*, for frying

1 clove garlic, peeled and finely chopped

1 mild chilli, finely chopped

1 x 400g *(14 oz)* tin of tomatoes or the equivalent weight of fresh tomatoes in season, peeled and chopped

200ml *(7fl oz)* water

1 tsp honey or brown sugar

1 tsp cider vinegar

½ tsp dried oregano or 1 tsp fresh oregano

1 large egg

sea salt, to taste

chilli flakes, to taste *(optional)*

toast, to serve

This has been a go-to brunch at weekends for me for years. Before I ever knew what shakshuka was, I was enjoying the simple, delicious joy that is eggs slow-poached in flavour-packed sauce.

One of the reasons I became so enamoured with them is that I could get the egg just right, with little drama. When you cook eggs in sauce with a lid on, the eggs will steam, ensuring a perfectly set white and, for me, a runny yolk. Perfect for a slow Saturday after a busy week.

You can make these eggs in any sauce. I love poached eggs in leftover curry or ragu too. A bright and fresh bacon-and-tomato sauce is perfect, though. Use a pan with a lid if you have one. If not, find an appropriate heatproof plate to cover the pan as the eggs cook.

I share this recipe for 1, you can double it for 2 in a regular size pan, or even 4. I cook brunch for one often, and I find a small 18cm (7-inch) frying pan indispensable.

METHOD

1. This is a one-pan dish so cook everything in it. Fry the bacon in oil over a medium-to-high heat and allow it to cook in its own rendered fat. When it is starting to brown, add the garlic and chilli and stir through for one minute.

2. Add the tin of tomatoes along with 200ml water (fill the tomato tin halfway with the water and pour in) and bring to the boil. Add the honey and cider vinegar (these balance the flavour of the tomatoes with a little acid and sweetness) and cook for 15 minutes. Add the oregano and stir through. Taste and adjust the seasoning.

3. Make space for the egg in the centre of the pan with a spoon or ladle and crack it in gently. Sprinkle some sea salt over the egg and, if you fancy it, some chilli. Reduce the heat to low, cover the pan and allow the egg to poach and cook in the steam gently until cooked to your liking.

4. Transfer to a serving plate and eat immediately, mopping up that gorgeous sauce and egg with your toast.

Bacon & egg breakfast tacos

INGREDIENTS

Serves: 3

For the tortillas *(makes 9 small tortillas):*

210ml *(7fl oz)* warm-to-hot water *(this will depend on your masa harina, so add the last bit slowly and you may need more)*

1 tbsp bacon fat

150g *(5½ oz)* masa harina *(maize flour)*

pinch of salt

For the Chipotle Salsa Rojo:

3 medium tomatoes, whole

water, for boiling tomatoes

1 tbsp of chipotle in adobo *(finely chop the chillies if not already a paste)*

½ red onion, peeled and chopped

2 cloves garlic

½ tsp ground cumin

sea salt, to taste

For the taco filling:

9 slices of bacon

6 large eggs

sea salt, to taste

6 tbsp grated cheese of your choice *(I like a good melting cheese for this, like Cheddar, Gouda or Gruyère)*

To serve:

fresh coriander

I was torn about this recipe from the beginning. I love tacos but did I want to include a recipe for a bacon and egg cheesy quesadilla instead, which I love just as much? Or a taquito! Crispy and gorgeous and stuffed with fluffy scrambled egg and crispy bacon. In the end I settled on the tacos, and even now as I type it, I wonder if I did the right thing. But tacos are always right, right? And these are cracking.

The key is making your own tortillas; they make it so much better. Homemade tortillas are fast and so tasty. Softer than any shop-bought ones too. Don't stress about a tortilla press, although you will likely want one once you have made them a few times and they become part of your regular rotation. Once you go down that road you can then start playing around with your homemade tortillas. Try filling a fresh raw tortilla with filling (including cheese) before folding and sealing to be fried as a Mexico City style quesadilla.

Fat is not traditional in a Mexican corn tortilla, although that is not to say that people don't do it. Adding a little of your stored liquid gold or freshly fried bacon fat adds a subtle flavour and textural difference that more than makes it worth the effort.

If you don't have chipotles for the salsa, use chillies of your choice or dried chipotles (toast them in a dry pan on both sides until fragrant first, then soak in boiling water for 20 minutes).

With thanks to Lily Ramirez-Foran of Picado in Dublin who first taught me how to make Salsa Roja!

METHOD

1. Prepare your tortillas. Add the water and bacon fat to your masa harina with a pinch of salt. Bring the mixture together with your hands until it forms a ball. If it feels dry or crumbly, add more water slowly. If it is too sticky, add a little more masa harina. Leave to rest under a tea towel.

2. Prepare the Chipotle Salsa Rojo while you let the tortilla dough rest. Cover the tomatoes with hot water from a kettle and boil until tender (approximately 15 minutes). Drain, saving some water to thin the sauce, and put the tomatoes in a blender with the rest of the Salsa Rojo ingredients. Blend and add water until you get a consistency that is thick enough but can still pour easily from a spoon. Season with sea salt to taste. Leave covered and set aside.

3. Get your tortilla press out and let's make our tortillas! If you don't have a tortilla press you can use a rolling pin, just be sure to put your tortilla dough between two sheets of greaseproof paper or similar. Line your tortilla press with a sheet of greaseproof paper top and bottom (I use a larger sheet folded in half.)

4. Divide the tortilla dough into roughly 9 equal-size pieces and roll each piece into a ball. Place each ball between the sheets of greaseproof paper in your tortilla press. Press flat and remove carefully. I like to press as I cook, as they can stick to each other when you let them sit in a stack for a while. I press as many as will fit in the pan (3 in a regular frying pan), and cook and press in batches.

5. Fry the tortillas in a dry frying pan (I like a cast iron pan for this, but use what you have). Fry for 1–2 minutes on each side until the edges start to dry and curl up. Remove to a plate and wrap in a clean tea towel while you prepare the rest, adding more as they cook. When they are all finished, store them well-wrapped in the tea towel where they will keep moist and warm while you prepare the bacon and egg filling.

6. To make your taco filling, chop the bacon into the same size as the rough width of the tortillas. Fry the bacon until crisp and remove to the side, keeping warm under foil or under another plate. Leave the fat in the pan and reduce the heat to low. Crack the eggs into a bowl and whisk until smooth. Season with sea salt and put into the frying pan with the bacon fat. Allow to cook gently until the edges are visibly cooked then pull the edges in and stir slowly. When the eggs are just before your liking, stir through the cheese and remove from the pan (they will continue to cook).

7. Serve your tacos with 3 tortillas per person topped with the cheesy scrambled eggs, bacon, Chipotle Slsa Rojo and some fresh coriander leaves.

Bacon sausage bread

INGREDIENTS

Makes: 8 slices

For the bread dough:

330g *(11½ oz)* bread flour

5g salt

100g *(3½ oz)* room
   temperature butter or
   lard

7g (¼ oz) fast-action yeast

3 large eggs

50ml *(2fl oz)* milk

For the bacon and
sausage filling:

15g *(½ oz)/*1 tbsp butter

1 red onion, finely
   chopped

400g *(14 oz)* sausage meat
   *(or the equivalent in
   sausages with the meat
   removed from the skins)*

1 tbsp fresh sage, finely
   chopped

6 slices smoked streaky
   bacon

1 egg for egg wash

sage leaves, to serve
   *(optional – they look
   great and are very
   tasty too)*

I love all of the recipes in this book of mine but I love this recipe so much. You absolutely need to make it. A soft bread dough, butter or lard and egg enriched with a little milk, so like a porky brioche but not as sweet and rich. You can use butter or lard, and if you have some bacon fat to hand, absolutely mix that in..

The bread is made in a more or less typical way, and proved twice. The second time you prove it is after you shape it as a sausage-and-bacon braid. Brushed with egg wash before baking, it gets a lovely bronze sheen.

For special occasions, double up the amounts and shape it into a circle. During the festive season you can fashion a bow of crisp-fried sage leaves and redcurrant berries and you have a Bacon Sausage Bread Wreath.

METHOD

1. Start by preparing your bread dough, using either a dough hook or by hand. It is important that your lard or butter is at room temperature, and therefore soft and easy to work with. This makes it much easier to mix.

USING A MIXER WITH DOUGH HOOK: Put all of the ingredients for the bread dough in your mixing bowl and mix at a low speed until it has formed a dough. If it feels sticky add a little more flour, a tablespoon should do it, but add more if you need to, slowly and mixing well every time. When it is no longer sticky but before it is dry and flaky, it is good. If it feels too dry, add a tablespoon of milk at a time (flours vary so both of these things can happen). Continue to knead with the dough hook for 5–6 minutes until the texture is no longer rough and it has an elastic quality.

BY HAND: the same as above but it takes longer to knead (approximately 10 minutes).

2. Cover the bowl with a clean tea towel and allow the dough to double in size in the warmest part of your kitchen or in your airing cupboard. This will be faster in the summer and slow in the winter; I usually put it near a radiator in the winter to help push it along. This proving stage usually takes an hour to an hour and a half.

3. Prepare your bacon and sausage filling. Melt the butter in a frying pan over a low heat and gently sauté the finely chopped red onion in it for about 10–15 minutes until soft, stirring occasionally. Allow to cool and combine with the sausage meat and sage and mix well with your hands.

4. When the dough has doubled in size, knock it back by punching the air out of it and allow it to settle for 5 minutes. Remove the dough from the bowl to a floured board and divide into three equal amounts. Roll into sausage shapes roughly twice the length of one of your smoked streaky bacon strips and just as wide. Flatten each log so that the width doubles and lay two strips of bacon on each so that the surface is covered with bacon from top to bottom. Now divide the sausage meat mixture into 3 and place the sausage meat on top of the bacon in a strip. Pull the dough up around the bacon and sausage meat gently and press it closed as best as you can and lay the three strips next to each other. Bread dough can take it, don't worry.

5. Join the three strips of dough together at the top and pinch them together so that they all orignate in the same place. Tuck the ends underneath what will become your loaf, and again, press them firmly underneath, without squashing the top, aiming to hide the messy bits and secure the braid. Braid the three strips by pulling the outside strand over the center one, and repeating with the other side until you have a braid. These look best if done a little tightly. Join the ends as neatly as you can, and tuck underneath, just as you did the start. Place on a baking tray lined with greaseproof paper and allow to sit at room temperature while you preheat the oven.

6. Preheat the oven to 200°C/180° Fan (400°F). Beat the egg and gently brush the surface of the braided bread with it. Bake your bread for approximately 25 minutes until golden brown. Best eaten warm and the leftovers (if any!) make a terrific French toast.

Bacon buttermilk waffles

INGREDIENTS

Makes: approx. 8 waffles

250g *(9 oz)* plain flour

1 tsp baking powder

25g *(1 oz)* brown sugar

good pinch of sea salt

2 eggs

475ml *(16fl oz)* buttermilk

50g *(1¾ oz)* melted butter

2 tbsp finely chopped
candied bacon
(optional; see p.198)

butter and/or rendered
bacon fat, to grease the
waffle iron

To serve:

3 slices streaky bacon, per
person *(or, you know, as
much as you want!)*

300ml *(10fl oz)* crème
fraîche

150ml *(5 fl oz)* maple
syrup *(you may want
more, who doesn't!)*

I ran a Sunday Bacon Club in London for a while. It was so much fun, we cooked several of my growing collection of bacon recipes, mainly sweets and jams, and then we ate brunch, which we also cooked. The recipes and food went down a storm. It was one of the inspirations for this book.

The highlight of the Sunday Bacon Club, even in the presence of Bacon Toffee, Bacon Fudge, Bacon Jam and Bacon Bloody Marys was always these waffles for me. Everyone gathered around a communal table and indulged in huge stacks of waffles served from a line of busy waffle makers with lots of bacon and maple syrup.

There is something so comforting about them, and they are so tasty too (of course!). The crispy fluffy waffle with the sweet-salty crispy bacon drizzled with maple syrup is pure comfort and joy. I love to add some crème fraîche on top for a little more indulgence, but this is up to you. And if you want, you can go double bacon, both in the waffle batter and on top, for those days when you really need that bacon pick-me-up.

As with all batters, this benefits from an hour's rest between completing the batter and making the waffle. If you can! If you can't, don't worry, they will still be good.

Can't have gluten? No need to panic! These work really well with gluten-free flour, as the egg brings the batter together and you don't do much to stretch that gluten besides! Substitute 225g (8 oz) gluten-free plain flour and 25g (1 oz) tapioca flour for the 250g (9 oz) plain flour and make sure you use gluten-free baking powder too.

1. Place all dry ingredients in a large bowl and mix well. Whisk the eggs with the buttermilk and add the melted butter. Slowly add the egg, buttermilk and butter mix to the dry ingredients, whisking gently as you do, until it just comes together. Take care not to whisk too much as it will lose lightness. Stir through the candied bacon, if using.

2. Leave the batter to rest for an hour, if you can. Even better, rest it overnight covered in the fridge. When you are ready to make the waffles, preheat your waffle iron. When hot, brush some butter and/or rendered bacon fat on the waffle plates. Per waffle, pour approximately a ladleful of batter in the waffle maker (this will depend on your waffle maker) and cook on high until golden. While the waffles are cooking, fry or grill the streaky bacon until desired crispness.

3. Serve the waffles hot, two per person with a generous dollop of crème fraiche, a few slices of bacon and a generous drizzle of maple syrup.

Bacon bloody mary

INGREDIENTS

Serves: 1

**For the bacon-fat
washed vodka:**

30g *(1 oz)* bacon fat

500ml *(18fl oz)* vodka

For the Bloody Mary:

wedge of fresh lemon
 (for the rim of the glass)

celery salt *(for the rim
 of the glass)*

60ml *(2fl oz)* bacon vodka

120ml *(4fl oz)* tomato juice

pinch of freshly ground
 black pepper

Worcestershire sauce,
 to taste

hot sauce, to taste

slice candied bacon
 (to garnish; see p.198)

The secret to a good Bacon Bloody Mary is, yes, serving it with a slice of crispy, chewy, sweet, salty, candied bacon, but also – and essentially – fat-washing your vodka.

I started making bacon vodka by frying fatty bacon and then pouring a bottle of vodka over it, leaving it for a few days and straining it before freezing it in a tub, so that the fat rose to the top (and was easy to remove) and then straining it.

This was completely delicious but felt quite wasteful and I thought there had to be a better way. I did some research and spoke to some bartender friends who told me that the trick was to wash the vodka in the rendered bacon fat only, as this is where all the flavour is. Sure enough, it works a treat.

The best and easiest way to do this is to save up your bacon fat every time you fry some bacon (which I highly recommend you do, anyway) and then when the time comes, or when you have enough, make yourself some fat-washed bacon vodka.

METHOD

1. To make the bacon-fat-washed vodka, warm through your bacon fat to loosen it and add it to your vodka. Mix well and let it sit for 8 hours or overnight. At this point the bacon flavour will be mixed throughout, but you need to remove the fat. The easiest way to do this is to put the vodka in a wide-topped container – like a large jar or a storage container – and put it in the freezer for a few hours. The fat will congeal and rise to the top, and you can just lift it out. Finally, to get rid of any further sediment, pass it through a coffee filter paper or similar. The bacon vodka will keep very well in the fridge for a couple of weeks.

2. To prepare your Bloody Mary, rub the top of your glass with the fresh lemon and dip it in the celery salt. In a separate glass, combine 60ml of the bacon vodka with the tomato juice, a pinch of black pepper, a dash of Worcestershire sauce and some hot sauce. Stir well and adjust the flavours according to your taste. Put some ice in the serving glass with the celery salt rim. Pour your Bloody Mary on top, taking care not to disturb the rim.

Optional: Mix it up by making a chipotle version
by adding chipotle hot sauce or with a small
amount of blended chipotles in adobo (to taste;
they can be hot, so start small). Horseradish is
another great seasoning option for those who like
things hot and spicy.

Bacon Bites

There had to be room for a chapter on satisfying bites, as bacon is one of the most satisfying bites in the world, just on its own. These recipes are for when you need a little of something really good, or a lot of something small and packed with flavour. Party bites to serve to and to share with friends or a tray of nibbles to accompany a night in front of the television. Whatever your requirements, I've got you covered with these bacon nibbles.

The recipes here are for smaller numbers than you might be catering for, but all are flexible and can be multiplied accordingly.

Cheesy bacon & tomato turnovers

INGREDIENTS

Makes: 6

1 pre rolled puff pastry
   sheet *(all-butter is best)*

6 slices bacon of your
   choice

150g *(5½ oz)* diced
   cherry tomatoes

75g *(2¼ oz)* finely grated
   mature Cheddar cheese

1 egg, beaten

sprinkle of mild chilli,
   to serve

These turnovers are as good as they are simple. They come together quickly and easily and make a perfect snack. You could also shoehorn these into brunch or a breakfast on the go.

A simple piece of shop-bought puff pastry cut to size and introduced to bacon, tomato and cheese. A little egg wash for polish and some herbs to finish. Ten minutes of your time, tops. So much satisfaction!

METHOD

1. Preheat your oven to 200°C/180°C Fan (400°F).

2. Cut the pastry into six roughly equal-sized rectangles. Turn the individual pastry pieces so that they are oriented in a diamond shape.

3. Put a slice of bacon on each from the top corner to the bottom. Add the tomatoes and cheese, dividing evenly between the 6 pastries.

4. Gently fold the sides over, one on top of the other and press down.

5. Brush the pastry with the beaten egg. Bake on a sheet of greaseproof paper for 18–20 minutes until golden brown.

6. Finish with a sprinkle of chilli and some finely cut chives. These are best eaten hot but are good cold too.

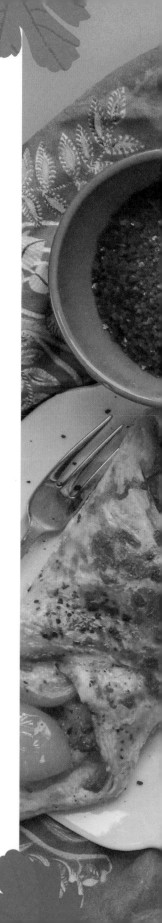

Bacon devilled eggs

INGREDIENTS

Makes: 6

60g *(2 oz)* bacon

6 large eggs, at room
    temperature

3 tbsp mayonnaise

1 tsp Dijon mustard

hot sauce, to taste

sea salt, to taste

2 spring onions, green
    parts only, finely sliced

chilli flakes or paprika,
    to garnish

Bring back the devilled egg, I say! Classic egg mayonnaise too,
while I am on the topic. Eggs and mayonnaise together are
a dream. Even better with bacon, as with (almost) every single thing.

Devilled eggs graced many a table in the '70s and '80s but then
disappeared, along with the cheese and ham pineapple hedgehogs
(yes, those!) and another precious thing, the vol-au-vent.

The devilled egg has enjoyed a recent small resurgence and it is to
be celebrated. I love them so much that I have dedicated devilled
egg plates at home (and no, that is not too much).

I often make devilled eggs as a snack just for myself, but they are
perfect canapés too. If you want to devil just one egg for yourself
for a snack, I would absolutely encourage it.

METHOD

1. Fry your bacon until crisp. Remove from the
heat and finely chop when it has cooled down.

2. Next: boil your eggs. Put the eggs in a pan
big enough to accommodate them comfortably.
Cover them with cold water and bring them to
the boil. Turn off the heat, cover the pan and let
the eggs cook for 10 minutes. The yolks will be
set but not chalky.

3. Remove the eggs from the hot water and run
under cold water in a colander or sieve until
cool (you can put them in ice water if you are
an organised person with ice). This will help
with peeling their shells. Peel the eggs, cut in
half lengthwise with a sharp knife, aiming to
get as clean a cut as possible.

4. Remove the egg yolks with a teaspoon and
put them into a mixing bowl, setting the cooked
egg whites aside. To the egg yolks, add the
mayonnaise, the chopped bacon, mustard,
a dash of hot sauce, a good pinch of salt and
half of the sliced spring onions. Mix well
until smooth and taste, adjusting seasoning if
necessary. If you want your final result to look
perfect, you can pipe the mayonnaise filling
back into the cooked egg whites. I generally
use a teaspoon and keep it simple and very
homemade-looking.

5. Finish with a sprinkle of chilli or paprika and
the remaining sliced spring onions.of bacon and
a generous drizzle of maple syrup.

Dates with bacon and blue cheese

INGREDIENTS

Makes: 16

16 toothpicks

16 large dates *(like Medjool)*

8 slices streaky bacon

90g *(3 oz)* blue cheese *(like Roquefort)*

16 blanched whole hazelnuts

Devils on Horseback are an essential part of the bacon culinary canon and a great snack. I had to include my take.

These are a treat. The depth of flavour, the sweetness of the date contrasting with the salty savouriness of the bacon, the texture contrast, the gently oozing blue cheese and that pop of hazelnut.

I make them two ways, with bacon inside and wrapped in bacon, both of which are in the photo. My preferred and most practical way is to give them a bacon cummerbund, as it helps keep the filling inside. I am sharing that recipe here.

As much as I love bacon, and while it is a central character in this small performance, it just has a supporting role. There are a few strong flavours here and they need to play well together. If you don't like blue cheese, feel free to substitute Brie or similar.

METHOD

1. Preheat your oven to 200°C/180°C Fan (400°F).

2. Soak the toothpicks in water while you prepare the dates.
If your dates still have stones in them, remove the stones carefully and discard. Tease the sides open gently with a sharp knife so that there is a pocket of each date to stuff.

3. Cut each slice of bacon lengthwise into two long halves.

4. Stuff each date with a teaspoon of the cheese and finish with a hazelnut tucked into one end. Wrap each date carefully with a strip of bacon and give them their bacon cummerbund. Secure with a toothpick.

5. Place the stuffed dates on a tray lined with greaseproof paper and roast for 10 minutes until the bacon is visibly crisp and the cheese is starting to ooze. Allow to cool a little before serving, but serve hot.

Beer battered bacon with chipotle mayonnaise

INGREDIENTS

Makes: 12

12 slices streaky bacon

For the beer batter:

200g *(7 oz)* plain flour

275ml *(9¼ fl oz)* beer
(*I like an IPA for this*)

good pinch of sea salt,
for seasoning

2 tsp baking powder

For the chipotle mayonnaise:

3-4 tbsp chipotle in
adobo, to taste *(finely
chop the chipotles if they
are whole; alternatively
use
dried chilli)*

200ml *(7fl oz)* mayonnaise

squeeze of lemon juice,
to taste

oil for deep-frying
(*any neutral oil, like
sunflower or rapeseed;
groundnut oil is
particularly good
for frying*)

You read this and just thought YES, right? Of course you did. Especially if you grew up on battered sausages and scallops (battered slices of potato) from local chip shops like I did.

Why haven't you been battering bacon all these years? I can't answer that for you, that is between you and yourself. We do have time to rectify this now and catch up, so let's get busy.

METHOD

1. Put the beer in the fridge for an hour before making this recipe. It is very important that the beer batter is cold. Why? It helps the batter stick to the food that you are frying. This is a trick that I learned from making tempura. If you are very serious and organised about it you will refrigerate your flour too.

2. Make the chipotle mayonnaise by mixing the chipotle in adobo with the mayonnaise and adding lemon juice to taste. Add more chipotle if you would like it hotter, less if not. Set aside.

3. You will need to prepare carefully for deep-frying. First: a pan to fry the bacon in – a deep-fat fryer is ideal if you have one, for temperature control and for safety. If you don't, a large, regular high-sided pan will do, but please be very careful and don't leave it unsupervised. A thermometer will help you ensure you get the temperature just right but if you don't have one, check the temperature by dropping some batter in the oil and when it immediately sizzles you are good to go. A wire rack with kitchen paper underneath is ideal for draining the bacon.

4. Heat your oil (the quantity depends on pan size, but your pan should be at least 2.5cm/1in deep with oil) to 190°C (375°F), and while the oil is heating, prepare your batter. Put the flour and salt in a large bowl and mix well together with the baking powder. Slowly add the cold beer, mixing gently. When it has come together, stop mixing. It is very important that you don't over mix it, which will result in a gluey batter.

5. One at a time, dip each strip of bacon in the batter and gently lower into the very hot oil, taking care not to overcrowd the pan, which will reduce the temperature. Fry in batches for a couple of minutes and turn each piece with tongs to make sure both sides cook evenly.
It should take approximately 4 minutes per piece. It is ready when the bacon is golden brown and crisp.

6. Drain the deep-fried bacon on a wire rack over some kitchen paper while you fry the remaining slices (or just drain on kitchen paper if you don't have a wire rack, but not for long as the bacon will get soggy underneath). Ensure your oil is brought back up to temperature before frying the remaining batches of bacon.

7. Serve the beer-battered bacon hot with the chipotle mayonnaise.

Bacon wrapped halloumi with tamarind tomato sauce

INGREDIENTS

Makes: 12

For the tamarind tomato dipping sauce:

2 cloves garlic, peeled and
    finely chopped

olive oil, for frying

1 x 400g *(14 oz)* tin
    tomatoes

1 tbsp honey

2 tbsp tamarind extract
    *(if unable to source, try
    equal parts brown sugar
    and lime juice)*

400ml *(13 ½ fl oz)* water

sea salt, to taste

450g (1lb) halloumi
    (roughly two packs)

12 slices streaky bacon

Halloumi is a wonderful cheese that cooks beautifully. I love it wrapped in bacon and fried with a punchy, tart, tamarind tomato dipping sauce. It also makes a wonderful component of a salad.

METHOD

1. Make the dipping sauce first. Sauté the garlic over a medium heat in 1 tbsp olive oil for a couple of minutes, stirring so it doesn't burn. Add the tin of tomatoes (break up the tomatoes with a spatula or wooden spoon if they are whole) with the honey and tamarind extract. Fill the tomato tin with water and add this to the pan also. Bring to the boil and reduce the heat to low. Cook for half an hour, stirring occasionally, so that the tomatoes break down and the sauce reduces slightly. Season to taste with salt.

2. While the sauce is cooking, prepare your halloumi. Cut each block in half lengthwise and then into 3 pieces each, leaving you with 6 pieces per block; so, a total of 12 halloumi pieces. Wrap each piece in bacon.

3. When the sauce is almost ready, heat a couple of tablespoons of olive oil over a medium heat in a large frying pan and fry the halloumi for a few minutes on each side until the bacon is crisp and brown.

4. Serve immediately with a bowl of the tamarind tomato dipping sauce on the side.

Bacon-wrapped jalapeño poppers

INGREDIENTS

Makes: 16

180g *(6¼ oz)* cream cheese

50g *(1¾ oz)* finely grated cheese like Parmesan, gruyère or humble cheddar works well too

sea salt, to taste

16 large jalapeño peppers

8 slices of streaky bacon, cut in half lengthwise *(a thinner-sliced bacon is better here)*

The first time I had these they were pulled from a friend's freezer as an emergency Christmas snack after we had returned from the pub. I have been hooked since, and of course as with most things, they are even better when cooked at home.

METHOD

1. Preheat your oven to 200°C/180°C Fan (400°F).

2. Combine the cream cheese and grated cheese and stir well.
Season to taste with a little salt.

3. On to the jalapeños. It is best to wear gloves when preparing hot chillies. Cut them in half down the centre with a sharp knife. Remove the membrane and seeds (unless you like them hotter), and then stuff each one with the cheese mixture. Wrap each jalapeño pepper with one of the half slices of bacon. Place on a flat tray covered with a slice of greaseproof paper, cheese side up.

4. Bake your jalapeños for 25–30 minutes until the bacon is crisp. Allow to cool slightly before serving, as the cheese will be very hot straight out of the oven.

Figs with mascarpone, blue cheese, honey and candied bacon

INGREDIENTS

Makes: 8

250g *(9 oz)* mascarpone
   cheese

100g *(3½ oz)* Gorgonzola
   *(or another mild blue
   cheese)*

2 tbsp honey

8 ripe figs

3 slices of maple candied
   bacon, chopped small
   (see p.198)

These are best when figs are in season in summer and perfectly ripe. They come together quickly and require no cooking, with the exception of the candied bacon, which you can make in advance.

METHOD

1. Combine the mascarpone cheese, Gorgonzola and honey and stir well.

2. Using a sharp knife, cut a cross through each fig to near the bottom, but not quite. Gently pull the edges of the fig apart and fill with the cheese and honey filling. Top with the candied bacon and serve.

Bacon and cabbage dumplings

INGREDIENTS

Makes: 24 dumplings

For the dumpling filling:

400g *(14 oz)* shredded cabbage *(use your favourite cabbage, mine is hispi)*

2 tsp fine salt

350g *(12 oz)* minced pork

100g *(3½ oz)* streaky bacon, minced or chopped very small

2 cloves garlic, peeled and finely chopped

2.5cm *(1 in)* ginger, peeled and grated

4 spring onions, finely sliced

1 tbsp sesame oil

1 tbsp cornflour

1 egg white

sea salt, to taste

For the dipping sauce:

100ml *(3½ fl oz)* soy sauce

100ml *(3½ fl oz)* Chinkiang black rice vinegar

chilli oil or laoganma *(chilli crisp)*, to taste

24 dumpling or gyoza wrappers

neutral oil for frying *(such as groundnut or sunflower oil)*

100ml *(3½ fl oz)* water, for steaming dumplings

This is one of a few nods to my Irish cultural and culinary heritage, and our obsession with bacon and cabbage. It combines this with my love for Chinese food, and especially dumplings.

You can get the dumpling wrappers in Chinese or Japanese shops. They are a very handy thing to have in your freezer. The Chinkiang black rice vinegar is a deeply flavoured beautiful Chinese vinegar, easy to source in Chinese shops and online. If you have not been acquainted yet, I am delighted to introduce you. It will become a firm friend in the kitchen. While you are stocking up, get some laoganma also, aka chilli crisp. Dried chilli and crispy fried onion in oil; it is perfect in the dipping sauce here and also with your breakfast eggs.

With thanks to Chef Ken Hom who taught me to add egg white and cornflour to my dumplings to make the filling lighter.

METHOD

1. Before preparing the dumpling filling, put the shredded cabbage in a bowl and put two teaspoons of fine salt on it. Mix well and leave to sit for half an hour, mixing with your hands occasionally. The salt will draw the water out of the cabbage and soften it. Put the cabbage in a clean tea towel and squeeze, wringing all excess water out of it. Discard the liquid.

2. Make your dipping sauce by combining the soy sauce and Chinkiang vinegar, then adding chilli oil or crisp to taste. Set aside.

3. For the dumpling filling, combine the pork, bacon, cabbage, garlic, ginger, spring onions, sesame oil, cornflour, egg white and a little sea salt. Mix well, best with your hands. Fry off a little bit to taste and adjust the seasoning if necessary. You may not need to, as there is salt in the cabbage and bacon.

4. When filling your dumplings, have a small bowl of water on the side that you can dip your finger into to wet the edge of the dumpling wrapper before you fill them. This will help seal the dumpling. Keep the dumpling wrappers in their pack or under a clean tea towel, so they don't dry out. The most common mistake that people make when they prepare dumplings is to overfill them so that they burst while cooking or even before they get to the pan. You will get a feel for this as you make more.

5. Hold a dumpling wrapper cupped in the palm of your hand (so as not to lose your money, as a Chinese friend explained to me). Wet the edge of it lightly and add just under a tablespoon of filling in the centre. Pinch the edges of the wrapper together. If you are not familiar with pinching the wrapper to get a nice shape and secure the filling, this is something you can practise and I recommend watching YouTube videos that teach this specifically. For now, just press the edges together securely and make sure they are tight and they will be fine. Put the filled dumplings on a flat surface and gently push them down so that they will get a flat bottom and sit comfortably as you cook them and on the plate. If they burst at this point it is usually because there is too much filling. You will get a feel for this very quickly.

6. Cook your dumplings in batches, using a frying pan with a tight-fitting lid. Heat a couple of tablespoons of oil in the pan over a medium heat. Add the dumplings when the oil is hot, flat side down, and as many as will fit in the pan. Fry until golden brown and crisp at the bottom, shaking the pan gently occasionally so that the dumplings don't get stuck. Add roughly 60ml/2 fl oz water and put the lid on the pan immediately (it will sizzle furiously when you first add it so take care). Cook until the water is almost fully absorbed, then take the lid off and continue cooking until there is no water left and the dumpling bottoms are crisp again.

7. Serve hot with the dipping sauce. Dumplings = deepest joy.

Feel-Good Comfort Food

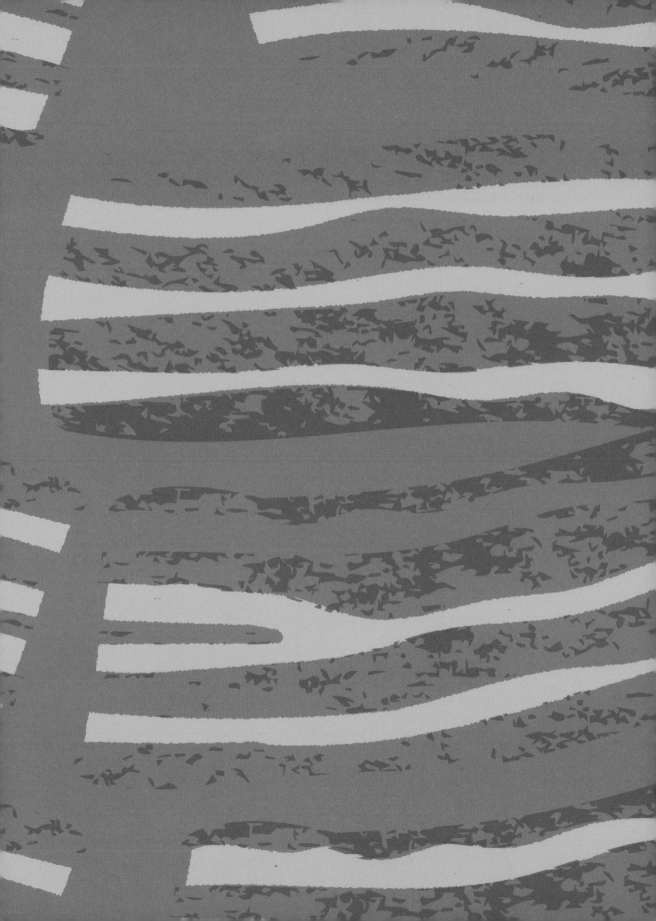

Feel-Good Comfort Food

Feel-good comfort food is the niche where I am most likely to be found on any given day. Or anything to do with snacks, aka Bacon Bites. Feel-good comfort food is necessary, and special.

I could wax lyrical about the importance of cooking at times when you really need something good and nice in your life. Cooking as an act of self-care. Cooking as a meditation. Cooking as nourishment of body and soul.

But let's not take our eyes off the prize. BACON.

A bite of bacon is immensely satisfying anyway, and immediately takes you to somewhere blissful. Then, when you base a complete comfort-food dish around it, you can go somewhere truly extraordinary.

Keywords here: cheesy, boozy, soupy, curry and carbs. Get stuck in. We have some comforting to do.

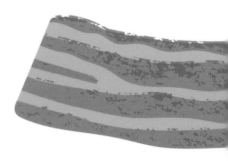

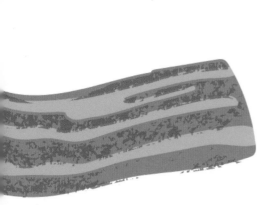

Buttermilk bacon wedge salad

INGREDIENTS

Serves: 4 as a side dish

200g *(7 oz)* bacon lardons, or sliced streaky bacon

For the dressing:

200ml *(7fl oz)* mayonnaise

100ml *(3½ fl oz)* sour cream

100ml *(3½ fl oz)* buttermilk

2 tbsp finely chopped chives

1 garlic clove, peeled and crushed

sea salt, to taste

To serve:

1 head iceberg lettuce, cut into quarters

150g *(5½ oz)* blue cheese *(like Roquefort)*

There is something cooling and soothing and oh-so-satisfying about this retro salad. Iceberg lettuce is much maligned, but it is a great vehicle for flavours and textures like these.

METHOD

1. Fry your bacon in a pan until crisp.

2. While the bacon is frying make your dressing by combining the ingredients and seasoning with salt to taste.

3. Drizzle the dressing over the iceberg lettuce and serve with the crumbled blue cheese and fried bacon lardons.

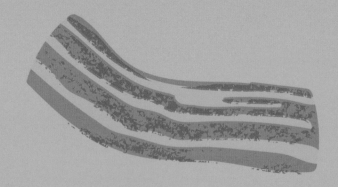

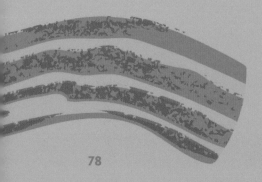

Cheesy bacon grits

INGREDIENTS

Serves: 4

1 litre *(1¾ pints)* water

pinch of sea salt

190g *(6¾ oz)* stoneground
grits

150g *(5½ oz)* bacon
lardons, or sliced
streaky bacon

4 spring onions, sliced

25g *(1oz)* butter

75g *(2¾ oz)* grated
mature Cheddar

hot sauce, to taste

parsley leaves, to serve

I bought a bag of stoneground grits on a trip to the
US some ears ago and I was hooked. It is compared
to polenta often, but it is different. You can see that
they are related, though. I buy grits online now in
the UK and always have a bag to hand for moments
that require deep comfort. Try and get the proper
stoneground grits. They take longer to cook, but the
instant ones just aren't the same.

METHOD

1. Bring the water to a boil in a saucepan with
a generous pinch of salt. Add the grits to the water,
stirring as you do. Reduce the heat to low and allow
to cook gently, stirring regularly. The grits will start
to thicken. When it gets to the texture of a porridge,
they are done. This will depend on the grits you use,
but it generally takes 45–50 minutes.

2. Fry your bacon lardons with the spring onions in
a pan when the grits are almost ready. Set aside.

3. When the grits are done, stir through the butter,
two-thirds of the cheese and some hot sauce (to taste).
Check for seasoning and add salt if necessary.

4. Serve the grits in a bowl with the bacon and
spring onions, parsley and the remaining grated
cheese
on top.

Bacon mac and cheese

INGREDIENTS

Serves: 4

300g *(10½ oz)* macaroni
  or elbow pasta

**For the bacon
cheese sauce:**

100g *(3½ oz)* smoked
  streaky bacon, finely
  chopped

30g *(1 oz)* butter

50g *(1¾ oz)* plain flour

500ml *(18fl oz)* whole milk

1 tbsp English mustard

300g *(10½ oz)* grated
  mature Cheddar cheese
  plus 100g *(3½ oz)*
  grated mature Cheddar
  cheese to sprinkle on
  top

sea salt, to taste

50g *(1¾ oz)* breadcrumbs

a little butter for greasing
  the dish

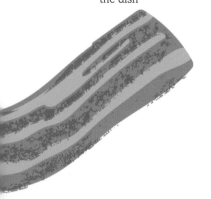

Sure, you can have mac and cheese without bacon, but why
would you? Bacon mac and cheese is actual code for comfort food.

I didn't grow up with mac and cheese. I discovered it as an adult and
embraced it with gusto. I keep this one simple, allowing the bacon to
shine and sing and shout, and do whatever bacon needs to do in that
moment that requires comfort.

You can go all fancy with the cheese but it is hard to
beat a good mature Cheddar, and so I stick with that here.

METHOD

1. Preheat your oven to 200°C/180°C Fan (400°F).

2. Cook your pasta according to packet instructions and when
it is cooked, refresh in cold water with a little oil to stop it sticking.

3. While the pasta is cooking, work on your sauce. Fry the bacon in
a pan over a medium heat until brown and starting to crisp. We want
to render as much fat out as possible, as we will use that as a base
for the cheese sauce.

4. Remove the bacon from the pan and put to the side, leaving the
fat in the pan. There should be over a tablespoon of fat in the pan,
if there isn't add more butter. We need a ratio of 50:50 butter and
flour to make a roux, which is the cooked flour and butter paste
that thickens the sauce. Add the butter to the bacon fat and when
it is melted, add the flour. Stir in and keep stirring until the mixture
turns a slight caramel colour. A whisk is best at this stage to keep it
moving.. You want to make sure that the flour is cooked through.

5. Add the milk a little at a time, ensuring it is incorporated into the
roux. It will absorb quickly. Roux is thirsty. When all the milk has
been added, reduce the heat and allow it to heat through and thicken
gently. Stir occasionally as it does. Add the mustard, cooked bacon
and the 300g grated cheese and stir through. Turn the heat off.
Check the sauce for seasoning and check if you need to add more
mustard.

6. Mix the pasta and the sauce and put into your buttered baking dish. I like to use a big dish to make a shallow mac and cheese with a larger crispy cheesy crust. Mix the 100g cheese and the breadcrumbs and sprinkle on top of the mac and cheese. Bake for 25 minutes or until the top is golden brown.

7. Serve immediately. Leftovers are great shaped into fingers or patties, breadcrumbed and deep-fried.

Bacon-wrapped sausage toad-in-the-hole

INGREDIENTS

Serves: 2

For the batter:

110g *(3¾ oz)* plain flour

½ tsp sea salt

2 medium eggs

300ml *(10 fl oz)* whole milk

For the gravy:

2 onions, peeled and
   sliced

1 tbsp oil

250ml *(8½ fl oz)* cider or a
   lighter beer

1 tbsp cornflour

400ml *(13½ fl oz)*
   chicken stock

sea salt, to taste

1 tsp fresh thyme leaves
   (removed from the stem)

6 sausages

6 slices streaky bacon

1 tbsp oil

How do you improve on toad-in-the-hole? It is simple. Wrap the sausages in bacon! (Cue the sound of an angelic choir).

For the uninitiated, toad-in-the-hole is a big Yorkshire pudding with sausages cooked into it. It's perfect. And if you've had a week that is too meaty or you fancy some veg, just wrap pumpkin or soy-marinaded aubergine (eggplant) wedges in bacon and substitute them for the sausages.

There are two secrets to a good toad: letting the batter rest for at least an hour; and making sure the fat in the baking dish is good and hot before you add the batter.

METHOD

1. Make your batter first. Combine the flour and half a teaspoon of salt in a bowl. Make a well in the centre and add the eggs, whisking gently, pulling the flour in from the side. Add the milk in a steady stream, stirring all the time. The batter should be of pouring consistency (quite runny but with a little thickness). Leave to stand for an hour at least. This is important and allows the glutens to stretch, so don't skip this. You can leave it in the fridge overnight and it will be even better. Whisk before you use.

2. Start your gravy by getting the onions on, as they will take time. Fry the sliced onions in 1 tablespoon of oil for about 30 minutes until soft and starting to caramelise. It is worth it, if even only for the smell. While the onions are cooking, we will get the toad in the oven.

3. Preheat your oven to 220°C/200°C Fan (400°F). Wrap each sausage with a slice of bacon and roast in the oven in a deep baking dish (approx. 24cm x 30 cm/9 ½ in x 12 in) for 10 minutes with a tablespoon of oil. Remove the baking dish from the oven and arrange the sausages so that they are evenly spaced. There should be plenty of fat from the sausages and bacon in here, which will kickstart the batter and also add lots of flavour. Whisk the batter then pour gently around the sausages and put the baking dish and

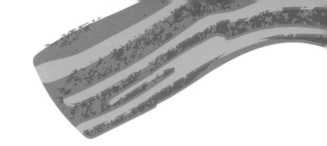

put the baking dish back in the oven. Bake for 25 minutes or until the batter is all puffed up and golden brown.

4. While the toad is roasting, finish your gravy. Add just a small splash of the cider to the cornflour and stir it until it is dissolved. Add the remaining cider and stock to the onions and bring to the boil. Reduce the heat to low. Add the cornflour-cider mix and stir through immediately as you add it. This will thicken the gravy slightly. Season with salt and add the thyme.

5. Serve the toad with lots of gravy. Proper comfort food! Enjoy.

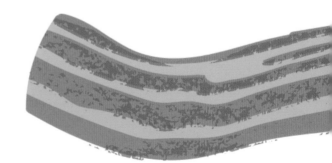

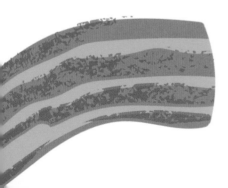

Boozy bacon clams

INGREDIENTS

Serves: 1

400g *(14 oz)* clams
   *(Palourde clams are a
   good choice)*

olive oil, for frying

100g *(3½ oz)* smoked
   bacon lardons/sliced
   streaky bacon

2 cloves garlic, peeled and
   finely chopped

1 large tomato, grated

200ml *(7fl oz)* dry
   white wine

finely chopped parsley,
   to serve

finely chopped chives,
   to serve

mild chilli flakes, such as
   Turkish pul biber or
   Korean gochugaru *(or
   your favourite!)*, to serve

sea salt, to taste *(optional)*

Clams may seem an unusual choice for comfort food but truly, they
are, especially when the juices are mopped up with lots of lovely
crusty bread. This is a dish I love to make just for myself but you
can multiply easily for friends.

METHOD

1. Before you start, discard any open clams that won't close
when you tap on the shell.

2. Heat 1 tablespoon olive oil in a sauté pan over medium heat. Add
the bacon and cook until starting to brown, about 5 minutes. Add the
garlic and stir for a minute, then add the tomato. Add the clams and
white wine and stir well. Continue to stir gently until all the clams
have opened. Discard any clams that have refused to open. Finish
with the herbs and chilli.

3. Check for seasoning before serving. This may not need salt with
the bacon and the brine from the clams, but I always include it in the
recipe and on the table, just in case.

Parmesan gnocchi with bacon and cabbage

INGREDIENTS

Serves: 6

For the Parmesan gnocchi:

1kg *(2¼ lb)* floury potatoes *(like Maris Piper)*, roughly the same size so they boil evenly

300g *(10½ oz)* plain flour

50g *(1¾ oz)* finely grated Parmesan cheese

½ tsp fine sea salt

1 egg

For the bacon and cabbage broth:

200g *(7oz)* smoked streaky bacon, cut into thin strips

2 red onions, peeled and cut into fine slices

3 cloves garlic, peeled and finely chopped

1 head of cabbage *(I like hispi, you can also use winter/spring greens)*, sliced

1 litre *(1¾ pints)* light stock *(such as chicken stock)*

sea salt, to taste

wild garlic/chive flowers or finely chopped chives, to garnish

I can't resist another nod to bacon and cabbage. Bacon and cabbage have been best friends forever; and in many countries, not just my native Ireland. The irony is that it was one of my most-hated dishes in childhood and I refused to eat it. The smell of the boiled cabbage was enough to drive me out of the house. But now, made my way, with cabbage cooked briefly and still verdant green, I adore it.

Gnocchi are very easy to make but there is a knack to it. As with many things that contain gluten, you want to get the gluten to stretch just enough, without overworking the dough, so that the gluten makes everything tight and chewy. Don't let that put you off. After a few times you will understand by feel what you are doing and looking for, and I will guide you here too. There is zero shame in buying gnocchi to make this also; I always have a packet in the cupboard for when I need something fast, and sprinkle the Parmesan on top after.

This will make enough gnocchi for 6 people. That may be too much for your purposes, but gnocchi freeze really well. Spread them out on a tray lined with greaseproof paper and put in the freezer. When frozen, put them in a freezer bag or and use them within a month. You can boil them directly from frozen. If you want to make this for 1 or 2 people, divide the ingredients accordingly.

METHOD

1. Boil your potatoes (whole, in their skins) until just almost tender. There should be a little resistance in the potato but you should be able to pierce them with a sharp knife. This way we ensure they don't absorb too much water.

2. While the potatoes are boiling, fry the bacon in a dry pan just in its own fat. After about 8 minutes, much of the fat will have rendered and the bacon will be browning. Remove the bacon with a slotted spoon, leaving the fat in the pan. Set the bacon aside. Add the red onion to the pan and cook over a low heat until soft for about 30 minutes, stirring occasionally while you prepare the gnocchi.

3. Peel the potatoes while still hot but cooled enough to handle. Discard the potato skins and pass the flesh through a potato ricer. If there are any lumps, pass them through a second time.

4. While the potato is still warm, add about two-thirds of the flour (the aim is to use as little of the flour as possible) with the Parmesan and salt and mix well. Beat the egg and mix this in. Lightness of touch really helps here; it is important not to overwork the dough. If the dough is still wet or sticky, add more flour, a little at a time. Once you get a soft ball of dough that is not sticky, you are done.

5. On a lightly floured surface, roll the dough into a log about 2.5cm (1-inch) thick and cut off small chunks to form gnocchi. To shape the ridges on the gnocchi and make the slight indent underneath, use the tines of a fork to press them lightly (or use a gnocchi board, if you have one). Place each gnocco on a lightly floured surface while you make the rest. Leave to sit for 20 minutes, this helps them dry out a little bit and they will cook better.

6. While the gnocchi are resting, let's work with our bacon and cabbage broth. Add the garlic, cooked bacon and sliced cabbage to the onions. Raise the heat to medium, and heat through for a few minutes, stirring as you do. The idea is to get the flavour of onions, garlic and bacon well-combined with the cabbage. Add the stock and bring the broth to just below the boil when it looks like it will start to bubble. Season with salt to taste and leave the broth over a low heat while we cook the gnocchi.

7. Bring a large pan of salted water to a boil. Reduce the heat to medium and cook the gnocchi. When they rise to the surface they are done, and you can add them to the broth.

8. Serve immediately. To garnish, I have used wild garlic flowers which were in season. You can also use chive flowers or finely chopped chives for the same flavour effect.

Cracklin' cornbread with jalapeño bacon beans

INGREDIENTS

Serves: 4

For the jalapeño bacon beans:

neutral oil, for frying *(such as groundnut or sunflower oil)*

2 onions, peeled and finely chopped

250g *(9 oz)* bacon lardons

3 cloves garlic, peeled and finely chopped

1 tbsp ground cumin

500ml *(18fl oz)* tomato passata

3 jalapeños, chopped

600g *(1lb 3oz)* home-cooked butter beans *(or 2 x 400g / 14 oz tins, drained)*

2 tbsp maple syrup

1 tbsp cider vinegar

300ml *(10fl oz)* water

salt, to taste

For the cracklin' cornbread:

320g *(11¼ oz)* cornmeal

1 tsp baking powder

½ tsp fine sea salt

50g *(1¾ oz)* plain flour

600ml *(1 pint)* buttermilk

2 large eggs

25g *(1 oz)* butter

100g *(3½ oz)* pork crackling or crispy fried streaky bacon, chopped into smaller chunks

fresh coriander, to garnish *(optional)*

Just the name Cracklin' Cornbread was enough to grab my attention. I assumed it was cornbread with crispy pork crackling cooked in it, and that was enough for me! But I was wrong, as cracklins are actually crispy fried pieces of pork fat (and you can, of course, use bacon). But I use crackling because I love it and it got in my head. If you are opposed to crackling, you can put crispy fried bacon in instead. I know you are not opposed to that as you are, after all, here.

Pork crackling is easy to source in the UK as a pub snack in shops and supermarkets. But if you aren't living in the UK, look for chicharrón in Latin American and South American shops. Chinese food shops will have it also.

Beans are somewhat of an obsession for me, I love them. They are a superb comfort food, they marry well with bacon, and are perfect with this cornbread. I pair them with jalapeño chillies here also. They have a gentle, bright heat. I grow a few jalapeño plants on my windowsill in summer. If you can't find fresh jalapeños you can use 2 tablespoons of jarred pickled jalapeños, and omit the vinegar from the beans.

I always make this cornbread in my small 23-cm (9-inch) cast iron frying pan. You can use a baking dish of a similar size.

METHOD

1. We will start with the beans. Heat 1 tablespoon of oil over a medium heat and add the onions. Stir through the oil and reduce the heat to low. Let the onions cook gently for 8 minutes, stirring occasionally, until they start to soften. Add the bacon and stir through. Cook gently until they start to brown.

2. Add the garlic, and ground cumin and stir through for a minute. Add the tomato passata, jalapeños, beans (if you are using tinned beans don't add them now or they will fall apart; add them at the end), maple syrup, cider vinegar, water, and a good pinch of salt.

3. Raise the heat and bring to just below the boil. Check for seasoning and add more salt if necessary. If it is a little sweet for you, add vinegar, and vice versa. It is all about balance, and not just here, but in every dish. Leave to cook gently while you make your cornbread. The sauce will reduce and thicken as it cooks. If it thickens too much, just top up with some freshly boiled water from the kettle.

4. On to the cornbread. Preheat your oven to 220°C/200°C Fan (425°F).

5. Put the cornmeal, baking powder, sea salt, and flour in a bowl and mix well. Make a well in the centre and add the buttermilk and eggs. Whisk them together and then pull in the dried ingredients until you get a smooth batter.

6. Put the butter in your cast iron pan or baking dish and put in the oven for a couple of minutes until melted. Brush the butter around the edges of the dish, taking care as the dish will be hot. Add the pork crackling or fried bacon to the cornbread batter and stir through. Pour the batter into the hot dish and bake until the cornbread is golden and firm to the touch (30–35 minutes).

7. Allow to cool, then remove the cornbread and cut into slices. You get a better consistency when you allow cornbread to cool. Serve with the jalapeño bacon beans and some fresh coriander leaves if you are using them.

Bacon and egg curry

INGREDIENTS

Serves: 2

4 large eggs

1 tbsp cumin seeds

12 black peppercorns

3 cloves

1 tbsp neutral oil *(such as groundnut or sunflower oil)*, for frying

1 onion, peeled and finely chopped

125g *(4½ oz)* smoked streaky bacon, cut into narrow strips

2.5cm *(1 in)* ginger, peeled and chopped/grated

1 hot chilli, chopped

2 tsp ground turmeric

3 cloves garlic, finely chopped

1 x 400g *(14 oz)* tin tomatoes

1 tsp brown sugar or honey

200ml *(7fl oz)* full-fat coconut milk *(light coconut milk just has extra water and less flavour)*

sea salt, to taste

1 fresh lemon

3 tbsp fresh coriander leaves

One day I added bacon and egg to a favourite treasured curried sauce and it was an absolute winner. I love an egg curry anyway, and find they are much underrated, even maligned, by people who mostly haven't tried them. I have tried many variations. A bacon and egg curry was the next logical step. One small step for me, one giant step for baconkind.

Needless to say, it's gone straight into the regular rotation, and hopefully it will become part of yours too. Serve with rice or the carb of your choice, because carbs are king and queen, just like bacon!

METHOD

1. Put the eggs in a pot and cover them with cold water. Bring to the boil, cover and turn the heat off. Leave them to cook in the residual heat for 10 minutes. Drain and refresh in cold water to stop them cooking (add ice, if you have it). Peel the eggs and leave to the side.

2. Toast the cumin and black peppercorns in a dry frying pan for a couple of minutes until fragrant. Remove from the heat and transfer to a pestle and mortar or spice grinder, and grind with the cloves. Set aside.

3. Heat 1 tablespoon oil in a shallow frying pan. Add the onion and fry until soft, about 8 minutes. Add the bacon and fry until starting to brown, stirring occasionally. Add the ginger, chilli, ground spices, turmeric and garlic and stir through. Cook for a couple of minutes, stirring continuously.

4. Add the tomatoes and the sugar. At this point with tinned tomatoes I would usually add vinegar too, but we will be finishing this with lemon juice, so it is ok as is. Bring to the boil, reduce the heat and cook for 10 minutes. Add the coconut milk and stir through until well combined. Leave to cook for a further 10 minutes. Check for seasoning and add salt if necessary. Squeeze the juice of half a lemon in, taste, and add more if necessary.

5. Back to the eggs! Slice them in half lengthwise with a sharp knife to get a smooth edge and place in the sauce. Put a lid on the sauce and leave the eggs to steam gently for a few minutes until heated through.

6. Add the coriander and a tablespoon of fresh lemon juice to the sauce to lift the flavour. Season and serve immediately. I serve this curry with brown basmati rice that's been rinsed, and cooked with twice the volume of salted water to rice. I frequently add a few cardamom pods, cinnamon cloves and some cinnamon bark to the rice while it cooks to lightly flavour it. It complements the cloves in the sauce.

Feeding Friends

Feeding Friends

Feeding friends is a joy and a pleasure. Informally only though, please. I don't subscribe to the idea of formal dinner parties. I prefer casual gatherings, served family style; where everyone sits where they like and wears what they like. Just a knife, fork and spoon. No formalities. Come as you are, bring a bottle of wine and bring a song, although if you are not Irish you might want to just point us to your playlist!

My favourite food to cook for friends is food that is first and foremost interesting and tasty. It also needs to come together easily so that I can manage my FOMO and ensure that I am right there in the thick of it much of the time. The last thing anyone who is feeding friends needs is stress in the kitchen. Uncomplicated dishes that are relatively hands-off or prepared in advance is the way to go. Let's keep the drama out of the kitchen and leave it to the politicians.

A bacon dinner or supper is a sure way to win friends over and have them beat a path to your door (friends who eat bacon, anyway!). These dishes will delight and surprise, comfort and soothe, each for their own different reason.

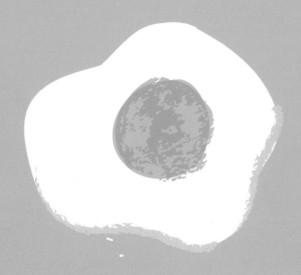

Pumpkin soup with bacon, sage and hazelnuts

INGREDIENTS

Serves: 4, as a starter or lunch

For the pumpkin soup:

2 red onions, peeled and finely sliced

1 tbsp olive oil, for frying

3 cloves garlic, peeled and finely chopped

750g *(1lb 3oz)* pumpkin or squash *(like Crown Prince squash)*, peeled and diced

1 litre *(1¾ pints)* chicken stock

150ml *(5fl oz)* single cream

sea salt, to taste

For the topping:

50g *(1¾ oz)* hazelnuts

100g *(3½ oz)* bacon lardons or sliced streaky bacon

12 sage leaves

When autumn hits, I get serious at my local farmers' market. I buy as many pumpkins as I can carry and I cook my way through them. Some are ideal served as wedges (Delicata squash: very sweet, but perfect with something sour), some I like to stuff (Onion squash) and others make great soups.

My choice for soup is a pumpkin or squash that has dense flesh that is full flavoured and rich, like a Crown Prince squash. Any culinary pumpkin will do, just avoid the carving ones. These are bred only for size and carving ability and taste like they might have met a pumpkin once and have a vague memory of it.

This soup is best served in a shallow bowl so the toppings don't sink.

METHOD

1. Sauté the sliced onions over a low heat in one tablespoon of olive oil until starting to soften, about 8–10 minutes. Add the garlic and stir through for a couple of minutes. Add the squash, and stock and bring to the boil. Reduce the heat and simmer. When the squash is tender (this will depend on your squash), add the cream and stir through. Season to taste and blend until smooth.

2. While the soup is cooking, prepare your toppings. Coarsely chop the hazelnuts until they are roughly chopped in half. Fry your bacon in a dry frying pan over a medium heat so that it cooks in and releases its own fat. When the bacon is golden and has rendered a lot of its fat, remove from the pan with a slotted spoon and keep on the side.

3. Fry the sage leaves in the remaining bacon fat for a minute or so, until the leaves have crisped. Gently remove them and keep on the side, separate from the bacon. Sauté the hazelnuts in the bacon fat until golden brown, add the bacon back in and stir through. Turn off the heat but leave them in the residual heat of the pan.

4. Serve the bacon and hazelnuts warm in a little pile on top of each bowl of soup and finish with the bacon-fat-crisped sage leaves.

Bacon beer cheese dip

INGREDIENTS

Serves: 4

150g *(5½ oz)* smoked
streaky bacon,
finely sliced

3 tbsp cornstarch

250ml *(8½ fl oz)* beer
(I like IPA here)

250ml *(8½ fl oz)*
evaporated milk

1 tbsp Dijon mustard

1 tbsp hot paprika

1 tbsp Worcestershire
sauce

1 tbsp hot sauce, plus
extra *(optional)* to serve

400g *(14 oz)* Cheddar
cheese, grated

sea salt, to taste

tortilla chips/crusty
bread, to serve

Beer and cheese are best friends, and beer and bacon are too.
It makes no sense not to bring them all together, and they work
fabulously well here.

There are so many different ways to approach a cheese dip, but one
of the easiest, fastest and best is to use evaporated milk as a base.
Best made before serving fresh, this comes together quickly.

METHOD

1. Fry the bacon in a dry frying pan until it's crisp and brown in
its own fat, about 8 minutes. Reserve the rendered bacon fat and set
the crispy bacon aside.

2. Combine the cornstarch with an equivalent amount of the beer
and mix well until dissolved. Keep on the side.

3. Combine the evaporated milk, remaining beer, mustard, paprika,
Worcestershire sauce, and hot sauce in a saucepan and cook over
a medium heat until hot and starting to steam.

4. Add the grated cheese, a good pinch of salt and the cornstarch
mixture and stir. When the cheese has melted, pour in the rendered
bacon fat and stir well. When the mixture has started to thicken
it is ready. Check the seasoning one last time and serve topped
with the crispy bacon and a splash of hot sauce on top and served
on the side. Some of us like a lot of it! Enjoy with tortilla chips
or crusty bread.

Scallops, bacon jam and tomato

INGREDIENTS

Serves: 1

3 scallops, trimmed

sea salt

olive oil and butter, for frying

half a lemon

3 tsp Bacon Jam, see p.202 for recipe *(and choose any one of them, they all work with this)*

2 cherry tomatoes, diced, to serve

fresh parsley, to serve

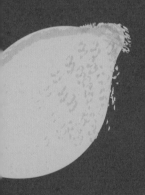

These look great and are so easy. Surf and turf with a different view. The sweet scallops go brilliantly with the intense bacon jam, which is a little sweet too but also tangy and big. The tomatoes bring a pop of fruitiness and acidity.

Which bacon jam? Entirely up to you. There are 4 to choose from and all will work really well here.

You can make the bacon jam in advance, leaving you with very little to do on the day but fry the scallops and chop the tomatoes. These are ideal as a starter, with a suggested serving of 3 scallops per person.

METHOD

1. Season the scallops with a sprinkle of sea salt on each side, and let them sit for 10 minutes before frying.

2. Heat 1 tablespoon olive oil and the equivalent of butter in a pan over a medium heat. Add the scallops and fry just a few minutes on each side until golden, basting with a spoonful of the oil/butter as they cook. Scallops should be cooked so that they are still tender in the middle, otherwise they get dry, so don't cook them longer than you need to. Finish with a squeeze of lemon.

3. Serve the scallops immediately with a teaspoon of bacon jam and some tomato on top of each one. Sprinkle chopped parsley and the remaining tomato on top and around the scallops.

Bacon chops with charred peaches, tomatoes and basil

INGREDIENTS

Serves: 4

50g *(1¾ oz)* flaked
   almonds

4 fruity beef tomatoes

extra virgin olive oil

4 chunky slices of
   sourdough

4 peaches, pits removed
   and halved

4 bacon chops

1 lemon

2 tbsp mild fruity chilli
   flakes, like Korean
   gochugaru or Turkish
   pul biber, to serve

handful of fresh basil
   leaves, to serve

sea salt, to taste

Bacon chops are a game changer. Easy and fast to cure at home (see p.218), and if you are lucky you will have a butcher nearby that sells them. Because they are seasoned all the way through by the process of curing, they don't dry out unless overcooked.

I love to make this in summer when peaches are in season and the days are long and bright. I serve them on a big platter with lots of basil scattered on top. Avoid very ripe peaches, as tempting as they are; perfect to eat fresh, they will fall apart when cooked, so look for almost-perfect peaches that still have a firmness. Tomatoes are in season at the same time. Pick big, fruity ones. I especially love fruity yellow or orange beef tomatoes here.

I will share a recipe for 4 people but make it for 6, 8, 12, or as many as you like, by multiplying the ingredients.

METHOD

1. Toast your flaked almonds first in a dry frying pan until golden brown. This happens quickly and they can burn, so keep an eye on them, and move them around. When done, set the toasted almonds aside.

2. Peel your tomatoes by cutting a large 'X' in the base and covering them in a bowl with boiling water for a minute. Drain and peel the skin off, starting at where you marked the 'X'. Cut out the top centre (where the stem was) and cut into 6–8 wedges, depending on the size of your tomato. Trust me, this is worth it, I won't ever suggest extra work that isn't absolutely necessary. If you don't remove the skin now, you will be picking it out of your teeth in 45 minutes' time and you will notice it while you are eating too. We can remove that awkwardness. Once you start peeling tomatoes you will do it all the time, even when you are eating alone at home in PJs. You can peel your peaches in the same way, but I like to keep the skin on. It looks and tastes good and doesn't bring the same level of drama.

3. Drizzle some olive oil over the bread and fry over a medium heat until golden brown on each side. Remove from the pan. Add more oil to the pan, as the bread will have soaked all that up, and char the tomatoes and peaches on each side for a few minutes, just long enough to brown them slightly.

4. Turn the heat up to medium high. Put the bacon chops on their side, fat side down, and press into the pan using tongs to sear the fat. You can do a few at a time. When the fat has crisped on the edges, cook the bacon chops on each side for about 3 minutes. This will depend on how thick your chops are, but you will know when they are done when they are firmer to the touch. Finish with a squeeze of lemon juice.

5. Tear the bread into course chunks and serve with the bacon chops, tomatoes, and peaches on a big plate to share. Finish with the toasted almonds, a sprinkle of chilli, a scattering of fresh basil, and sea salt. Serve while the bacon chops are hot.

Chicken, bacon and cider pie

INGREDIENTS

Serves 4

3 leeks, ends removed and finely sliced

olive oil and butter, for frying

125g *(4½ oz)* smoked bacon lardons

750g *(1lb 10oz)* skinless, boneless chicken thighs, diced into chunks

250ml *(8½ fl oz)* cider

200ml *(7 fl oz)* chicken stock

few sprigs of thyme

250ml *(8½ fl oz)* crème fraîche

1 sheet all-butter puff pastry *(approx. 320g/11¼ oz)*

1 egg, beaten, to glaze

I love a pie. Yes, this is comfort food, but a big pie to be shared with friends needed to be included in this chapter.

I recommend indulging your creative side/inner child by decorating your pie with the pastry offcuts. I like to make alphabet letters and spell out in pastry what is in the pie. You can even put a message on your pie. A pig cutter is also a valuable thing to have when you are making lots of bacon things and it is the star of the show. Some shapes like stars are lovely too.

Pies like this often start with a roux but I like to keep this lighter. The pastry is just on top, so it is not like it will get soggy, and you get a gorgeous creamy filling underneath

Shop-bought pastry is absolutely fine, and you can use white wine here too, if you prefer that to cider.

METHOD

1. This starts with the leeks. It is important to let them braise very gently for at least 15 minutes so that they soften and offer up some sweetness. It is a total transformation and only requires a little of your attention. Heat a tablespoon of oil and the equivalent of butter over a low heat in a high-sided frying or sauté pan. Add the leeks and stir through, ensuring they get coated with the butter and oil. Braise gently over the lowest heat, stirring occasionally, for 15 minutes.

2. Add the bacon and cook for a further 5 minutes, then add the chicken. Stir through and cook until it has transformed from raw to white all over. Add the cider and the stock with the thyme leaves stripped from the stems, and raise the heat. When almost at the boil, turn the heat down and leave to cook for 15 minutes. The liquid will have reduced, and we will now thicken it further by adding crème fraîche for a little luxury and some freshness.

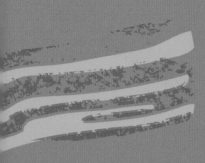

3. Preheat the oven to 200°C/180°C Fan (400°F). Butter your pie dish (a 26cm/10-inch one is best, or making individual pies can be lovely too), and add the pie filling. Take your pastry out of the fridge just before you need it. Add any pastry decoration on top, if adding, then brush with the beaten egg. Bake for 25–30 minutes or until the pastry is gorgeous and golden. Serve immediately.

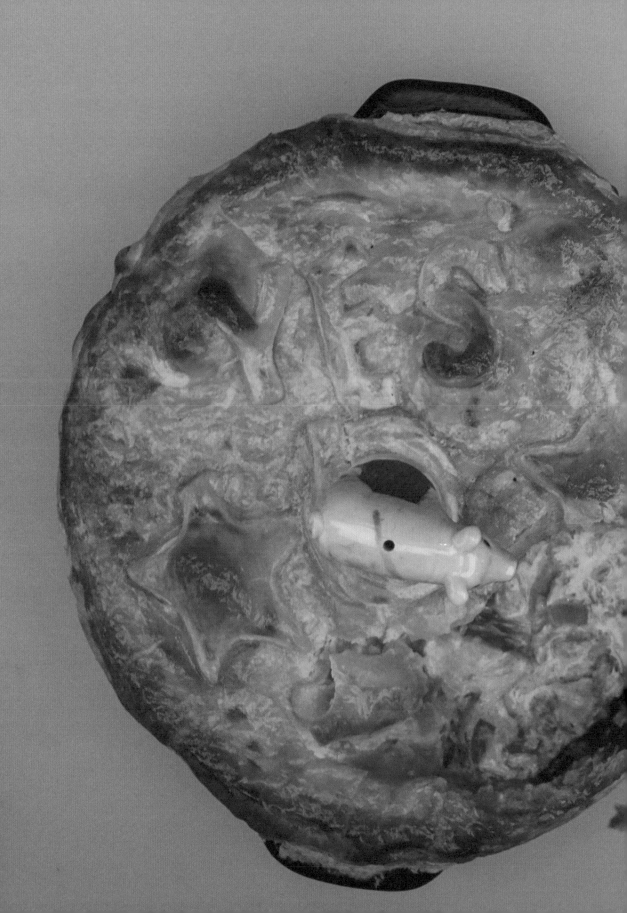

Bacon-wrapped pumpkin with chard, feta, chilli oil and toasted pumpkin seeds

INGREDIENTS

Serves: 4

800g *(1lb 11¾ oz)* pumpkin, seeds removed and cut into wedges *(aim for 12 wedges)*

12 slices of smoked streaky bacon

extra virgin olive oil

50g *(1¾ oz)* pumpkin seeds

sea salt

200g *(7 oz)* chard *(spinach or kale will do here too)*

4 chunky slices of sourdough

3 tbsp chilli oil, to serve

400g *(14 oz)* feta cheese

I love this dish. Bacon doesn't dominate here, but it is most certainly in the room. It is like the secret security detail for the pumpkin, wrapping the gorgeous, sweet, roasted pumpkin and giving it a crisp tasty jacket. Feta adds a creamy sharpness, chilli oil a brightness, and toasted pumpkin seeds a lovely crisp contrast. We eat our greens here not just because we should but because we love them! They bring everything else together.

Choose a great flavoured pumpkin or squash for this. I like Crown Prince squash, as with the soup earlier. Check out your local markets in autumn to see what they have and, of course, use whatever you can get if there is a limited selection available. You can eat the skin of most pumpkins and squashes. I tend to leave it on.

In terms of the seeds, I prefer shop-bought green pumpkin seeds for this; they are nicer and easier to eat. Compost the ones that are in your pumpkin (unless you really like those ones, then fire away).

METHOD

1. Preheat your oven to 200°C/180°C Fan (400°F).

2. Wrap each pumpkin wedge in bacon and place on an oiled tray. Drizzle with olive oil and roast until the pumpkin is tender and the bacon is crisp, about 30 minutes, depending on your pumpkin and how thick you have cut them.

3. While the pumpkin is roasting, prepare the rest. Toast the pumpkin seeds in a dry frying pan until they puff up and start to pop (aside: these make an excellent snack, so maybe make extra!). Sprinkle with sea salt and leave to the side.

4. Cut the chard into 2.5cm (1-inch) wide strips, and cook gently in a pan with some olive oil and some sea salt until just wilted and still bright green (prepare this towards the end of the pumpkin cooking time, just prior to serving).

5. Drizzle your sourdough with some olive oil and fry until golden brown on both sides. Tear into chunks just before serving.

6. When the pumpkin is ready, arrange it on a serving plate, family style, with the wilted chard strewn around, torn chunks of the toasted sourdough, a drizzle of chilli oil, crumbled feta and the toasted pumpkin seeds. Serve while the pumpkin and chard are hot.

Roast bacon-wrapped hake with white beans, preserved lemon and rosemary

INGREDIENTS

Serves: 4

sea salt

800g *(1lb 11¾ oz)* fillet of hake

10 slices of bacon *(enough to cover the hake, so have more bacon on hand in case you need it, thin sliced streaky is best)*

900g *(2lb)* home-cooked white beans *(or 3 drained 400g/14oz tins)*

4 Beldi preserved lemons, chopped into small dice, pips removed

few sprigs of rosemary, stems removed and finely chopped

extra virgin olive oil

200ml *(7fl oz)* dry white wine

1 fresh lemon

Bacon wrapped around a fish is not new, but it is very good, especially with a lovely tender fish like hake. Hake is beloved in Ireland and Spain, and rightfully so. It is a beautiful, flavoursome white fish that flakes tenderly when cooked. It is paired with meats often, like chorizo and bacon.

This is an easy roasting-tin dish to share with friends and family. Preparation is minimal and the rewards are large. It looks great and it tastes better. Preserved lemons are completely gorgeous and suit the fish, beans and bacon so well. You can make your own, but I prefer to buy the Beldi lemons in jars. They are small with thin skin and a superb flavour.

I say 'white beans' because literally any white bean will do. I like butter beans for this, and plump, enormous Greek gigantes beans when I can get my hands on them. Love chickpeas? Go right ahead, throw them in.

Beans are best home-cooked, and not necessarily on the day, unless you have the time. I batch-cook them when I can and freeze them in 300g (10½ oz) portions, roughly the equivalent of a tin. Home-cooked beans always seem like an ordeal, but they cook themselves and you do virtually nothing. It just makes sense if you love beans as much as I do.

Ask your fishmonger to get in a large hake for you and to fillet it. You can use monkfish too. This recipe can easily be adapted for a solo supper or for two.

METHOD

1. Lightly salt the hake a couple of hours before you cook it and keep it covered in the fridge.

2. Preheat your oven to 180°C/160°C Fan (350°F).

3. Remove the hake from the fridge and wrap it in the bacon, ensuring that the ends of the bacon finish underneath and won't be visible. You can do this as one larget centrepiece, or you cna make individual portions. Gently mix the beans, preserved lemons and rosemary with the white wine in a roasting dish big enough to accommodate them. Season with sea salt and add add a good splash of extra virgin olive oil. Stir through.

4. We will roast the fish at the same time, but separately, on a greaseproof paper lined roasting tray of its own, so that the bacon can roast nice and crisp. Drizzle a little extra virgin olive oil on top of the bacon-wrapped hake before it goes in the oven.

5. Roast for 20-25 minutes or until the bacon is looking golden and crisp.

6. Squeeze some fresh lemon juice over the hake, taking care to remove any pips. Put the bacon-wrapped hake on top of the beans, in the roasting dish or on a serving plate. Serve straight from the roasting dish with a serving spoon.

Roast bacon loin with cider and fennel cream cabbage

INGREDIENTS

Serves: 4

1kg *(2¼lb)* bacon loin, skin removed if there is skin on it

500ml *(18fl oz)* bottle dry cider

1 large cabbage *(savoy works well here)*

1 tbsp sea salt, plus more to taste if needed

1 tbsp/15g *(½ oz)* butter

3 cloves garlic, peeled and finely chopped

1 tbsp fennel seeds

1 tbsp cornflour + 1 tbsp water

100ml *(3½ fl oz)* crème fraîche

handful of fresh parsley leaves

This is the first of two recipes that roast whole slabs of bacon, one loin (unsliced back bacon) and one belly (unsliced streaky bacon). It is an entirely different thing to cook bacon this way in terms of texture and taste, and it makes a great centrepiece or part of a bigger meal when feeding friends, or just anyway.

A note on roasting a slab of bacon: traditional old-school bacon used to be very salty, and so it was recommended that it was soaked before it was used. This belief remains in some places, but most modern bacon is a lot less salty and is almost always ready to eat.

It is always best to check though, especially if you intend to slice it thicker, and if you haven't cured your own. So, slice off a chunky bit and fry it to taste. If it seems too salty, soak it for a few hours and try it again.

Again, this is a nod to bacon and cabbage, but here in grand design. The bacon roasts in cider and the cabbage is cooked on the hob with garlic, fennel seeds, more cider and cream.

As with everything in this book, this recipe is completely adaptable. I have also made it with 2kg (4½ lb) bacon loin for more people, and you can keep multiplying. It's a cracking dish. The bacon loin stays gorgeously moist and the flavours are fresh and lively, but also comforting.

METHOD

1. Preheat your oven to 180°C/160°C Fan (350°F).

2. Take the bacon loin out of the fridge 30 minutes before roasting. Put it in a high-sided roasting dish just a bit bigger than the loin. Pour all of the cider around the loin, ensuring it is covered and cover with foil or a lid.

3. You can relax for the first 30 minutes of oven-roasting time. Pour yourself a glass of wine, have a cup of tea. Just stare out the window, it is such a nice thing to do and we live in a world where we just don't take the time to do it anymore. Back to the kitchen 30 minutes later though.

4. Roast for 30 minutes, remove the foil and roast for 20 further minutes uncovered. Remove from the oven and rest the bacon under foil for 10 minutes. Drain the cider, which is now bacon-flavoured cider glistening with bubbles of bacon fat and flavour.

5. Slice the cabbage finely with a sharp knife. Heat the butter in a large shallow pan or frying pan over a medium heat. Add the garlic and stir through. Cook for a couple of minutes. Add the cabbage, some salt and the fennel seeds and stir well. Add about 125ml, or a regular wine glass full of the roasting juices to the cabbage. Add the crème fraîche, and stir through. Adjust seasoning to taste. I like to keep the cabbage fresh and lively but cook it to your taste, of course, if you like it softer.

6. Pass the remaining cider and bacon juices through a sieve into a separate saucepan and bring to the boil, reducing it as much as you can while the bacon rests. Add 1 tablespoon each of honey and cider vinegar. Taste and add more of the cider vinegar and/or honey if required, this will depend on the flavour profile of your cider. Dissolve the cornflour in the water first by stirring it vigorously until smooth, and quickly whisk it in to the sauce to thicken it a little. Check seasoning and adjust if required.

7. I like to serve the bacon sliced on top of a bed of the cider-and-fennel creamed cabbage on a big plate, family style or in a nice oven dish straight from the oven, with that gorgeous sauce on the side. Finish with the parsley leaves.

Chipotle cola bacon slab

INGREDIENTS

Serves: 8

2 whole dried chipotle
chillies

1 litre *(1¾ pints)* cola

2 cloves garlic

2kg *(4½lb)* whole bacon
slab *(bacon belly)*

Now, this. When I first made this recipe I expected it to be great, but it was even better. It is a nod to Nigella's famous Ham in Coca-Cola, which is where I was first introduced to the idea. It turns out that ham in cola is really popular in the southern US where Coca-Cola is based.

It makes perfect sense to do it. Cola is both sweet and acidic and so it makes a superb marinade. I do this one slightly differently to the norm because I love roasting bacon, although of course you could boil the bacon in cola too. This makes a terrific alternative to a Christmas ham, and your friends will love you even more if you serve this to them.

You can leave the skin on the ham if there is skin on yours, as per the photo, but it isn't necessary; and if you do, remove the skin before serving, as it can be chewy. I recommend using 2kg (4½lb) of bacon here, even if you are just making it for a few people, as the leftovers are phenomenal. You can cut the leftover bacon into chunks and make a delicious brunch the next day or add it to chilli bean soup. Or cook it further until you can pull it apart and serve it with nachos!

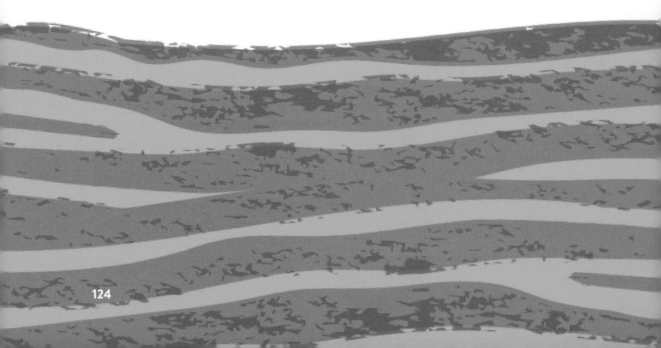

METHOD

1. Peel the garlic and chop it into rough chunks. We just want the flavour and we will remove it before serving.

2. Toast the chipotle chillies on both sides in a dry frying pan until fragrant (a couple of minutes on each side). Bring the cola almost to the boil at the same time and add the chipotles to the cola You can chop the chillies after 20 minutes if you want that flavour dispersed throughout, or even blend them with the cola.

3. Put the bacon slab in an ovenproof dish that fits the bacon and that will accommodate the cola marinade. It is important that the marinade covers the bacon, so don't use a dish that is too big. Pour the chipotle-garlic-cola over the bacon, cover and leave it in the fridge overnight.

4. Take the bacon out of the fridge 30 minutes before you plan to roast it.

5. Preheat your oven to 180°C/160°C Fan (350°F). Cover the bacon with foil (or a lid if the dish has a lid) and put the bacon in the oven for 30 minutes. Remove the lid/foil and put the bacon back in the oven for a further 20-30 minutes, depending on how thick your bacon is.

6. Remove from the oven and allow the bacon to rest under foil for 10 minutes. The sugar from the cola will ensure that the bacon is very hot. While the bacon is resting, remove the cola-chipotle-bacon juice joy from the roasting dish and add 2 tablespoons of cider vinegar. Transfer to a wide shallow pan like a frying pan and heat over a high heat to reduce the volume and concentrate the flavour.

7. Serve the bacon in slices with a little bowl of the chipotle cola and bacon juices (to dip the bacon in. Make sure you hide some of the leftovers from everyone else or you won't get any.

Bacon BBQ

There is no doubting that bacon has a special place on the BBQ. It can form a crispy shield from the heat, protecting what is inside and allowing it to cook more gently, all the while adding bacon fat and flavour and that crisp texture too. It is irresistible and that is why people like me write books about it.

People who love BBQ are obsessed, which is something that people who love bacon have in common with them. Of course, the overlap between the two groups is enormous, and BBQ websites are packed with bacon recipes like the Bacon Explosion. I love the enthusiasm and the hunger that leads to a recipe like this, but it's not my thing. My take on bacon and cooking is different: I focus more on bacon as an ingredient and an enhancement.

The joy of bacon ribs and bacon chops is something I want to cover here. These cuts of pork are traditions in my native Ireland, although you don't see ribs as much now as before. They are easy and relatively quick to make yourself. Bacon curing isn't difficult, it just requires precision weighing scales, a little care and time (as covered in the Bacon Curing chapter on p 202).

It would be remiss of me not to make some suggestions in the intro here that don't warrant a full recipe page of their own. These are often the best things. Great ingredients intersected with simplicity, reaping large rewards. Something a little different is always great too.

Peaches wrapped in bacon cooked on the BBQ are divine, particularly when in season. For this, choose peaches that are ripe but slightly firm so that they don't fall apart on the grill. Peaches and bacon are two parts of a wonderful flavour trinity, the third part being habaneros. Ripe habaneros can be hard to come by, but you could use a Habanero sauce. Too hot for you? Go milder, it's your food, and you should adapt it to your taste.

We can also bring the bacon and cabbage passion to the grill. Grilled cabbage is gorgeous. I surprised a friend with it recently and he was completely blown away. Brush cabbage quarters with oil or, even better, bacon fat, and cook it for a few minutes on each side until charred. I like sweetheart or hispi cabbage for this, quartered lengthwise. I suggest serving it in the style of the Buttermilk Bacon and Blue Cheese Wedge Salad on p.74, but using grilled cabbage in place of the iceberg lettuce.

Let's get stuck in!

Bacon BBQ Sauce

INGREDIENTS

Makes: approx 600ml (20fl oz)

200g *(7 oz)* smoked streaky bacon, cut into narrow strips

100g *(3½ oz)* brown sugar

300ml *(½ pint)* tomato ketchup

100ml *(3½ fl oz)* cider vinegar

100ml *(3½ fl oz)* water

1 tbsp Worcestershire sauce

2 tbsp mustard powder

1 tbsp paprika

1 hot chilli *(if you have chipotle in adobo, these are great here too)*

sea salt

So, yes, I can see you raising an eyebrow at me, that IS a lot of sugar. BBQ sauce is sweet, and mine isn't even the sweetest by a long shot. The important thing in a good BBQ sauce is getting the balance right. Sweet, sour, spicy, hot, and deep. My taste leans to sour, so you might feel that you need to tweak this to suit your own. Which you absolutely should. I give you the recipe, and you adapt it, that is how it goes.

METHOD

1. Fry the bacon over a medium heat in a dry frying pan in it's own fat until it is golden brown. Add the sugar and stir in. Keep stirring until the sugar dissolves in the fat and the heat. Add the rest of the ingredients, except the sea salt, and stir in. Raise the heat and bring to just before the boil. Reduce the heat and cook for 10 minutes. Taste to check for sweetness, sourness and salt. Adjust by adding more sugar or vinegar, if required. The salt in the bacon may mean you don't need to add any sea salt.

2. Let cool for 5 minutes to reduce the risk of burns (speaking from experience, fat and molten sugar are a dangerous combination!) and blend it until smooth. You can store this in the fridge for approximately 5 days, although it's so delicious I find it doesn't last that long. You can freeze portions also in a suitable airtight container for 3 months and use it as you desire it.

Bacon BBQ rub

INGREDIENTS

Makes: your choice!

Equal parts of:

ground cumin

chilli powder

mustard powder

smoked paprika

garlic powder

celery salt

brown sugar

This is not a rub that has bacon in it, although I did try that! This is a rub that is superb on bacon, which you would then grill on the BBQ.

My suggested ways of using it are to put it on some thick-sliced streaky bacon, bacon chops, bacon ribs, and small bacon cubes cut from a slab of bacon. Basically, all of the bacon, all the time.

Once you have put the rub on the bacon, let it sit in the fridge for a while, overnight preferably, before grilling it.

METHOD

1. Combine equal parts of the ingredients to make your rub. Mix them well and store them in an airtight container.

Note: It goes without saying that if you feel a favourite spice of yours is missing here, adapt, adapt, adapt! Let me know too. I would love to try it.

Red-eye bacon ribs

INGREDIENTS

*Serves: 1 as a main meal,
or 4 as a side dish*

For the marinade:

500ml *(18fl oz)* freshly
brewed coffee

3 chipotles in adobo plus
3 tsp of the adobo
sauce
*(or substitute with
regular chilli)*

80ml *(2¾ fl oz)*
cider vinegar

4 tbsp rich brown sugar
(like molasses sugar)

4 cloves garlic, peeled
and finely chopped

generous pinch of
sea salt

1 rack of bacon ribs (I like
the meaty spare ribs
and have used them
here, but baby back ribs
are great too)

Bacon ribs are fabulous, and they are easy and fast to cure (see p.218). Baby back ribs cure faster than the meatier spare ribs from the belly. I like to cure both, depending on the time I have and what I plan to do with them. Baby back ribs are smaller and have less meat
on them, but they are also perfect for snacking on at a BBQ.

'Red-eye' refers to the coffee in the marinade, and the tradition of red-eye gravy in the US made with coffee or cola. As someone who struggles with sleep, this really spoke to me and inspired this recipe.

It is up to you if you want to share these or save them for yourself.

METHOD

1. Blend all of the ingredients for the marinade until smooth. Add to the bacon ribs and marinade in a container with a lid in the fridge for at least 2 hours, preferably overnight. Next, choose your cooking method.

TO COOK ON THE BBQ:

2. These are best cooked low and slow on the BBQ until tender. Wrap the ribs in foil with some of the marinade, saving the remaining marinade in the fridge to make a sauce. For low and slow cooking, aim for 110°C/225°F and cook the ribs for a few hours until they are tender.

3. When the ribs are almost ready, bring the marinade to the boil in a pan on your hob/stovetop, lower the heat and reduce the sauce until it coats the back of a spoon. Check the seasoning and adjust salt, sweetness (sugar) and sour (vinegar) to taste.

4. Remove the ribs from the foil carefully and brush the ribs liberally with the sauce. Put them directly on the hottest part of the grill so that they caramelise a little. Turn them to ensure that both sides get access to the heat and that they caramelise evenly, applying the sauce regularly with a suitable brush. The ribs will be done when glistening and smelling sweet, about 3-4 minutes each side, depending on how hot your grill is. Serve with the remaining sauce on the side as a dipping sauce.

TO COOK IN THE OVEN:

If you don't have a BBQ, or don't care for it, but want these ribs, I've got you. You can make these in the oven too. After following step 1, above:

2. Preheat your oven to 150°C/130°C Fan (300°F). Put the ribs and marinade in a high-sided tin and cover with foil. Roast gently for approximately 2 hours, basting with the juices every 30 minutes. Remove the foil, baste again, and roast for another 30 minutes.

3. Rest the ribs for 5 minutes under foil before serving. Pour the remaining reduced marinade in the dish over the ribs before serving, or serve the marinade in a small bowl on the side as a dipping sauce.

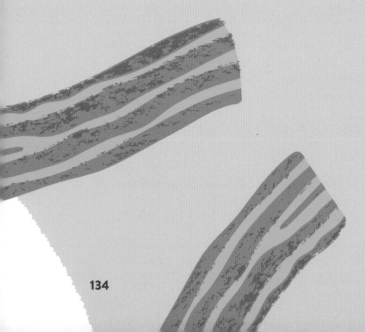

Bacon-wrapped pineapple

INGREDIENTS

Makes: 12 pieces

4 tbsp Bacon BBQ rub
(p.132)

1 fresh pineapple

12 slices of smoked
   streaky bacon *(+ extra if
   you cut the pineapple into
   more pieces)*

12 cocktail sticks,
   pre-soaked in water

chilli flakes *(I like Korean
   gochugaru for this, but
   use your favourite)*

Here I am, wading by choice into the pineapple-on-pizza row. I don't like saccharine oversweet tinned pineapple on pizza. I do love fresh pineapple coated in my spice rub and then wrapped in bacon and grilled until crisp and golden. It is so good.

METHOD

1. Put the BBQ spice rub on a plate and shuffle the plate so the flavours of the rub are evenly distributed.

2. Preparing a pineapple can be a pain, but it is worth it. Cut the top off, and cut a small slice off the bottom so that it will stand comfortably on a chopping board. Cut the skin off carefully by slicing it off with a sharp knife top to bottom. Pineapples have a hard core that we don't want to eat, so cut wedges off the side of the pineapple vertically, rotating it, so that only the core remains when you are finished. Discard the core and aim for 12 wedges of pineapple; if you have more, that is fine. Just use more bacon.

3. Dip each piece of pineapple in the BBQ spice rub, wrap the bacon around it and secure with a cocktail stick. Next, choose your cooking method.

TO COOK ON THE BBQ:

4. Cook the pineapple on the BBQ, turning it so that both sides caramelise, until the bacon is crisp and golden. Serve with a sprinkle of chilli. They will be very hot, so let them cool a little before serving.

TO COOK IN THE OVEN:

4. Follow steps 1–3 above, and pre-heat your oven to 180°C/160°C Fan (350°F). Place the bacon-wrapped pineapple pieces in a single layer on a greaseproof-paper-lined tray and roast for 20–25 minutes until the bacon is crisp and brown. Serve with a sprinkle of chilli.

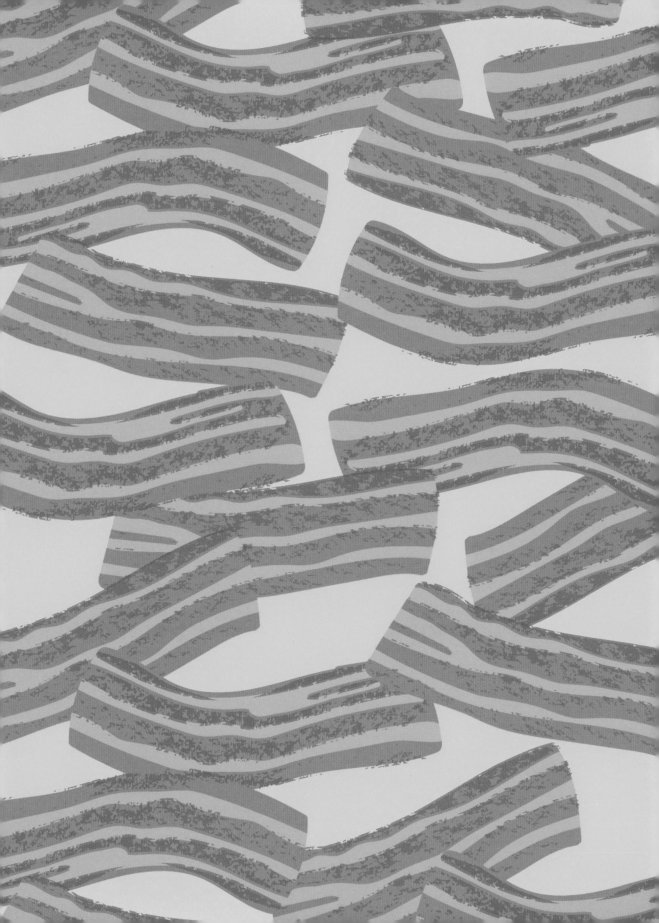

Bacon piri-piri spatchcock chicken

INGREDIENTS

Makes: 600ml (20fl oz)

For the piri-piri sauce:

50g *(1¾ oz)* paprika

50g *(1¾ oz)* cayenne pepper

250g *(9 oz)* smoked streaky bacon, sliced into strips

3 red peppers, stem and seeds removed

3 red chillies

1 red onion

250ml *(8½ fl oz)* cider vinegar

100ml *(3½ fl oz)* honey

juice of 1 lemon

sea salt, to taste *(optional)*

1 chicken

sea salt

some beer or cider in a spray bottle

salad/flatbread/chips, to serve *(optional)*

A spatchcock chicken is a treasured thing in my kitchen. You get succulent juicy chicken, and you get it faster. What can be wrong with that?

This piri-piri recipe is based on one that I got from chef Bertus Basson in Stellenbosch, South Africa. It is a rich, deeply flavoured sauce. Of course, I adapted it to include bacon, and the results were superb, so here it is.

This marinade recipe will make enough for a few chickens. It will keep in the fridge for 5 days; you can freeze it for up to 3 months too.

METHOD

1. Toast the paprika and cayenne in a dry frying pan for a minute, or cook it wrapped in foil in a hot oven (200°C/180°C Fan/400°F) for 5 minutes.

2. Fry the bacon over a medium heat in a dry frying pan until golden (about 8 minutes).

3. Combine the bacon and all of the rendered fat (this is key for flavour) with the rest of the piri-piri sauce ingredients and blend until you have a smooth marinade. Season to taste with salt (it may not need any, it depends on how salty your bacon is). If possible, it is best to leave the marinade sit at least overnight in the fridge to allow the flavour to settle.

4. You can ask your butcher to spatchcock your chicken for ease and convenience. If you need to do it yourself it is easy, and best with poultry scissors, which I absolutely recommend you have in your kitchen for every purpose. I use mine all the time. Put the chicken breast side-down and cut either side of the backbone. Remove the backbone, turn the chicken over and press flat. Season with a little salt. Rub the piri-piri marinade on and store your chicken covered in the fridge for at least 2 hours, overnight if you can.

5. When it comes to time to cook the chicken on the BBQ, remove it from the fridge 30 minutes ahead of time. Cook initially on the hottest part of the BBQ, skin-side down, and then turn over. Spray the chicken with the beer or cider occasionally as it cooks to keep it moist and to add flavour. Allow to cook gently until the chicken reaches a temperature of 74°C (165°F), as read with an instant-read thermometer, or when you check the flesh between the thigh and breast, you will see that it is white and feels firm.

6. I love this served with a salad and flatbread, or the ever-reliable homemade chips.

Brown sugar bacon kebabs

INGREDIENTS

Makes: 6 skewers

**For the spiced
brown sugar rub**:

200g *(7 oz)* soft brown
   sugar *(demerara sugar,
   if you can't source it)*

3 tbsp smoked paprika

1 tbsp fennel seeds

1 tsp ground black pepper

1 tbsp fine sea salt

500g *(1lb, 2 oz)* smoked
   bacon belly slab
   (unsliced streaky bacon),
   diced into 2.5cm *(1-in
   cubes)*

6 kebab skewers
   *(if they are wooden,
   soak them for at least 20
   minutes in water)*

This is really candied cubes of bacon with paprika and fennel. Candied bacon has several appearances in this book, each time warranted. On this occasion we are going to make a bacon skewer with diced cubes of sweet spiced bacon. You won't be sorry I told you!

METHOD

1. Combine all of the ingredients for the spiced brown sugar rub in a large bowl and mix well. Put the diced bacon in the bowl with the rub and massage in.

2. Thread the bacon cubes on to the skewers, leaving some space between each one so they can caramelise well. Place them on a tray, cover them and put them in the fridge for at least an hour.

3. Remove the skewers from the fridge 30 minutes before you want to cook them. You can cook these over medium-high or low heat, depending on how much time you have. These are best cooked on a piece of foil to retain the sugars and ensure that the bacon caramelises. Turn the skewers occasionally, and carefully, with a pair of tongs.

4. Cook until the bacon is cooked through and looks shiny and glazed. On a hotter BBQ or the hotter part of your BBQ, this will take approximately 20 minutes. You can also roast these in your oven at 180°C/160° fan (350°F) for 20–25 minutes, turning halfway through.

Cheese-stuffed bacon beef burgers

INGREDIENTS

Makes: 4 burgers

400g (14 oz) fatty minced beef

100g (3½ oz) smoked streaky bacon

100g (3½ oz) mature Cheddar, cut into chunks

sea salt

These are easy and gorgeous. The secret to a good burger is not just good meat, but meat with enough fat in it (you want 20% fat). Fat brings flavour and moisture to the burger. I put the bacon in the food processor and chop it small, you can do this with a knife too. I did buy a meat grinder to see if it was worth the purchase and the effort. I didn't use it enough to justify it, and I am sure you wouldn't, either. Streaky bacon has a lot of fat too, which will only help the burger along

Make sure the cheese is well-sealed by the burger patty or it will leak out while cooking and that would be a very sad thing indeed.

METHOD

1. Combine the beef and the bacon and mix well, kneading it for a few minutes in a big bowl so that it sticks together.

2. Divide the mixture into 4 portions and shape into balls. Put a ball in the centre of your palm and, using your fingers, make a deep dent in the centre. Put a quarter of the cheese in the dented space and close the meat mixture over it carefully. Press it down reasonably flat, making sure the cheese is secure inside. Repeat for the remaining 3 balls, put them on a covered tray and put it in the fridge for 1 hour so that the burgers will firm up.

3. Cook on a medium-high heat setting on the BBQ, salting the burgers a little just before and as you cook them. Remember that the bacon is salt also. These are both important details. Cook until the meat is browned on both sides and the burgers are still juicy.

BBQ bacon and chilli corn on the cob

INGREDIENTS

Makes: 4 portions

4 corn on the cob

100g *(3½ oz)* smoked
   streaky bacon, sliced

50g *(1¾ oz)* butter

2 chillies, finely chopped

2 cloves garlic, peeled and
   finely chopped

sea salt, to taste

fresh coriander, to serve

250ml sour cream, to
   serve on the side

chilli flakes, to garnish

3 lemons, 1 cut in half
   and 2 cut into wedges

Corn on the cob is a must for the BBQ. It loves a lick of flame and it adores bacon, butter and chilli. So, I add all these things here.

You can do this completely on the BBQ, but it will take a lot longer. It is easier to parboil in advance and finish over the coals. You save time and a lot of hovering and that has to be a winner.

Feta works really well crumbled over corn, especially with our magical flavour packed butter-bacon concoction that we create here. Feel free to add it as an extra. Grated parmesan cheese works really well too.

METHOD

1. If your corn has leaves, that is great. Pull the leaves back and remove the stringy bits. Tie the leaves back with some string, so it looks like a corn-leaf ponytail. Put the corn cobs in a large pot of boiling salted water standing up, so that the corn is completely covered but the leaves are outside the water. If your corn has no leaves you can just boil them. Either way, boil them for 10 minutes.

2. Fry the bacon in a dry frying pan in it's own fat until it is browning. Remove the bacon and add the butter, chilli and garlic to the bacon fat. Stir well and pour into a serving bowl to serve with the corn.

3. When the corn is ready, finish it on the BBQ to get that BBQ flavour. Brush the chilli-garlic-butter-bacon fat on the corn as it cooks, with just the fat only, reserving the bits for serving on top later. Turn it regularly until it is gently charred all over.

4. Remove the corn from the BBQ to a serving plate and sprinkle the bits from your magical flavour packed butter-bacon concoction on top, along with a sprinkle of chilli. Serve immediately with any remaining chilli-garlic-butter-bacon fat, coriander & the sour cream.

Bacon-wrapped scallop skewers with maple-cider vinegar glaze

INGREDIENTS

Makes: 4 skewers

12 scallops, trimmed

6 slices smoked streaky
  bacon, cut in half
  lengthwise

6 wooden BBQ skewers,
  soaked for 20 minutes

6 spring onions, ends and
  rough tops removed,
  cut into 2.5cm *(1-in)*
  sections

olive oil

**For the maple-cider
vinegar glaze:**

200ml *(7fl oz)*
  cider vinegar

100ml *(3½ fl oz)*
  maple syrup

Scallops again, but they are such a friend of bacon and the BBQ that
they had to make another appearance: this time, as these gorgeous
decadent skewers.

METHOD

1. Wrap the scallops in the bacon and thread the bacon-wrapped
scallops on the skewers: 3 per skewer, separated by a couple of
pieces of spring onion. Brush with a little olive oil.

2. Prepare your glaze by boiling the cider vinegar and maple
syrup in a pan, then lowering the heat and cooking it gently until
it is reduced by a third and is more viscous (you want to be sure
that it won't just run off the skewers).

3. Cook the bacon-wrapped scallops until the bacon is crisp on each
side. Don't overcook them or you will dry the scallops out. Put the
skewers on a serving plate and, using a tablespoon, carefully spoon
the glaze over the scallops. Serve hot.

Bacon
is Sweet

Bacon is Sweet

Bacon especially loves sugar and goes so well in confectionery. Bacon is a big fan of butter and cream too. Bacon is a bit of a boozehound. It loves most spirits, and here I pair it with bourbon, whiskey and rum.

This is likely the chapter that perplexes people the most. It is also my favourite chapter and in many ways the heart of what the book is about and where it started. I was making traditional fudge from scratch in my kitchen one day years ago. I had previously candied some bacon and it was sitting on a plate next to the hob (stovetop). I wondered what would happen if I combined them? And that was it. It was so good it sparked an exploration of bacon sweets.

Whatever you feel, I encourage you to explore this joyful bacon sweet shop. Make bacon sweets for yourself and for friends. Some of the recipes take longer than you might expect but they are absolutely worth the effort.

I know some of you will need a little encouragement, so if you only make three things from this chapter, choose Candied Bacon Fudge, Bacon Chocolate Toffee and the Bacon Krispie Marshmallow Bars.

Several of these recipes require the use of a thermometer to measure the sugar temperature precisely. If you don't already have a thermometer, they are a worthwhile investment. You can use them to roast meats and cook steaks just as you like them, and I wouldn't be without mine now.

Most of these recipes make great gifts (the ice cream might be tricky!) and you can make up your own box of sweet bacon treats for friends and family. I can tell you from experience that they will love it! (Unless, of course, they don't eat bacon).

A small note on the recipes! For recipes that require candied bacon, I list maple candied bacon. I do this because it is just simple candied bacon. If you have already raced to the Bacon Pantry chapter (p.182), you will see that you have a few other candied bacon choices and you can play around with these too if you prefer.

Candied bacon fudge

INGREDIENTS

Makes: approx. 20 pieces

4 slices *(100g / 3½ oz)*
   candied bacon *(p.184)*

100g *(3½ oz)* butter

300ml *(½ pint)* milk

325g *(11½ oz)* white
   granulated sugar

1 heaped tbsp golden
   syrup *(or corn syrup,
   see note above)*

60g *(2 oz)* brown sugar

4 slices of smoked streaky
   bacon

Homemade fudge might have been the first time that I realised that you could make sweets at home. Our childminder at the time showed me how to make fudge and toffee and I became obsessed. I started to make it all the time but I became frustrated with the process, as I rarely achieved a consistent result. It always tasted great, as caramelised sugar and butter always will. It was the texture that was an issue. Sometimes it was like toffee, sometimes it was squidgy and similar to – but not the same as – fudge.

As a teenager, when I was making Turkish delight in the microwave (yes!), I decided to embark on this caramel-coloured road to pleasure again. Grateful as I was for my childhood lessons, I decided to do some research so that I could figure it out. I had at this point learned about how jam worked and learned about sugar melting points. I could see now that my toffee issues were all about temperature.

Managing temperature and being precise with ingredients is what making fudge and toffee and all confectionery is about. It requires patience and precision. I have taught this recipe in many Bacon Masterclasses and at my Sunday Bacon Club. I see how people can lose patience and faith (usually at the same time). Then I see how thrilled they are when they finally produce bacon fudge. Sometimes people think this doesn't work, but this recipe is a precise science. Just follow the steps and you will be good.

None of this is intended to discourage you, quite the opposite. Steal a quiet part of a quiet day, make yourself a nice warm drink, stick on a podcast or an audiobook and embark on making homemade fudge, which is surely one of the finest meditations.

Using a large and wide high-sided sauté pan works really well here, as the water evaporates from the milk faster, meaning you can make your fudge faster. You can use a large pan too, just make sure the sides are high, as the milk will bubble up once it hits boiling point. This recipe can take some time, depending on your pan, but it shouldn't take more than 30 minutes. It may take longer initially if you are being very cautious, which is good.

Once mastered, this is so good you will want to hide it from yourself, in my experience. People are often judgemental of the idea at first, then curious and finally obsessed. Candied Bacon Fudge is gorgeous on its own, but it is sublime served on the side of a good whiskey, bourbon or rum. You can also add some bourbon, whiskey or rum to the recipe with very good effect.

Important note – the temperatures for cooking liquids are in Celsius and not Fahrenheit, which may seem silly to say, but I have had feedback from two people who burned their honeycomb from my previous cookbook, Comfort & Spice. It turned out they were measuring in Fahrenheit. You need to be accurate with the quantities for confectionery too, so please use weighing scales. It is important to use white granulated sugar for confectionery, not brown sugar. Brown sugar has impurities in it and does not melt or acquire candy characteristics in the same predictable way.

When making confectionery it is also important to use an invert sugar like golden syrup. Invert sugar is simply sugar that is broken down to its constituent parts. Using inverted sugars in confectionery-making improves the quality by preventing the crystallisation of sugars and it also improves the shelf life.

I use golden syrup because I like the flavour a lot and it is very easy to source in the UK. If you can't get it you can substitute honey, liquid glucose (which you will find in the baking section of most supermarkets) or corn syrup. You can make invert sugar too, if you become obsessed with home confectionery, as I did.

METHOD

1. Make your candied bacon first (as per p.198). When cool, chop finely and leave to the side.

2. Put all the ingredients, excluding the bacon, in a pan and bring gently to the boil over a medium heat, stirring gently and occasionally with a wooden spoon. Yes, we are about to boil milk, which likely goes against everything you have ever been told and maybe brings back traumatic memories of scorched boiled-over milk from a forgotten pot in the kitchen. We are managing this, so it will be ok. We have to go through 100°C to get to our fudge temperature of 116°C, so a kitchen thermometer is highly recommended

3. Once the milk starts to boil and very quickly starts to rise, move your pan so that it is halfway off the hob/stovetop (unless you have induction) and immediately turn the heat to low. Continue to cook the mixture, stirring occasionally and paying particular attention to the edges where sugar can get stuck and caramelise faster, and potentially burn. This can happen all along the bottom but once you keep an eye on it and stir the bottom occasionally and gently, scraping the bottom of the pan with your wooden spoon as you do, it will be fine. If it does happen, it is not a cause for panic, just stir it in, it is just caramel, and refocus your attention on the pan. It is important to start measuring the temperature now, not constantly, but every now and then until you are close to the end. When measuring the temperature, make sure the thermometer is not touching the pan, which will be hotter. Measure from the middle centre of the mixture in the pan.

4. You will notice that your fudge mixture will start to turn beige and, as it thickens, it will start to resist the spoon as you stir. This is what you want. The sugar is caramelising and the water is evaporating from the milk (we are essentially making a kind of evaporated milk here). The rise to the last 4°– 5°C is exciting and a little frustrating.

5. The magic number is 116°C. That is the 'soft ball' stage, which is when the sugar is hot enough to give the structure and slight firmness that we need in fudge, while retaining some softness. The soft ball stage can be 112°C to 116°C, but I prefer to err on the higher side, both for flavour and to reduce the risk of making a fudge that doesn't set. From 118°C we are heading into candy territory, so it is important to be precise.

6. Once you have hit 116°C, stop stirring, take the fudge off the heat and let it cool for a few minutes. Then stir for a good 5 minutes, until the fudge loses its sheen and starts to pull away from the side of the pan as you stir it. Don't be tempted to do this in a blender or food processor, you will just get (admittedly very tasty) crumbs. Stir through the candied bacon and pour into a 15cm x 15cm (6 in x 6 in) tin lined with greaseproof paper.

7. Leave to cool at room temperature and cut into squares to serve. Store in an airtight container. Fudge keeps very well and can be stored at room temperature; it is generally advised not to put it in the fridge, as this is dehydrating. There is bacon in this though, albeit preserved with sugar and fat. So, I recommend storing it in the fridge for up to a week in an airtight container lined with greaseproof paper. I have done it many times and it works well. Fudge also freezes very well, up to 3 months. If freezing, wrap it in greaseproof or wax paper before placing in an airtight container.

Butter toffee with candied bacon and chocolate

INGREDIENTS

*Makes: approx. 20
(but if you are going
to attack this with a
hammer, and you should,
I can't be too exact)*

10 slices *(250g/9oz)*
candied bacon

235g *(8¼ oz)* white
granulated sugar

150g *(5½ oz)* light
brown sugar

250g (9 oz) butter

1 tbsp/15g *(½ oz)* golden
syrup or honey

150g *(5½ oz)* dark
chocolate, finely
chopped

Homemade toffee is a joy. So buttery and gorgeous. It requires precision and a thermometer, as making fudge does, but because it is just butter and sugar and there is no milk to reduce, toffee comes together a lot faster: 10 minutes fast!

Cooking any confectionery makes your kitchen smell divine, but the butter toffee is very special. I don't stress about tempering the chocolate because life is way too short for that. We just want great candied bacon toffee with lovely chocolate on top, right?

A note on this one as before: it is important to use white granulated sugar for confectionery, not brown. Right! Let's get stuck in.

METHOD

1. Make your candied bacon first, as per p.198. Chop finely and leave to the side. Line a medium-sized shallow tray with greaseproof paper in preparation for your toffee.

2. Make your toffee. In a clean shallow pan – a heavy pan is best – heat your sugar, butter and golden syrup or honey. Once the sugar is melted, stir occasionally, ensuring that the bottom and the sides aren't catching. When the toffee starts to change colour from bright-yellow butter to golden, start keeping an eye on the temperature (ensuring you stir gently as you go). The temperature will start to climb very quickly so keep a close eye on it.

3. When the temperature hits what is known as the 'hard crack' stage, 148°C (but not higher than 154°C), turn the heat off immediately, and quickly and carefully take the pan off the heat. Pour the toffee very carefully and quickly into the ready-waiting lined tray (toffee sets very speedily, so it is important to be fast). Lift the tray gently and move it around so that the toffee pours evenly (again, carefully – this is so very hot). A lot of 'carefullys', but I am a clumsy cook and have suffered toffee and honeycomb burns, so learn from my experience rather than create your own story.

4. Scatter the chopped chocolate on top and spread it with a knife. The heat of the toffee will melt it. Sprinkle the chopped candied bacon on top and leave to solidify before cutting with a knife. Store it in an airtight container and enjoy. As with the fudge before, this is especially good served with a nice whiskey, bourbon or rum.

5. This will keep in an airtight container in the fridge for 5 days. You can freeze it in an airtight container too; just wrap it in greaseproof or wax paper first.

Bacon bourbon chocolate brownies

INGREDIENTS

Makes 8 brownies

125g *(4½ oz)* butter, plus extra for greasing

325g *(11½ oz)* dark chocolate

225g *(8 oz)* sugar

3 large eggs, at room temperature

50ml *(2fl oz)* bourbon *(you can also substitute rum or whiskey)*

100g *(3½ oz)* flour

1 tsp baking powder

pinch of sea salt

6 slices *(150g/5½ oz)* of candied bacon *(see p.198)*, finely chopped

There are as many brownie recipes as there are people. This is one of mine. It is a grown-up brownie recipe that is sticky with bacon and booze and rich with dark chocolate. Even if you take the booze out, kids generally don't go for it. So that is great for you parents, isn't it?! A kid-proof brownie recipe. Older kids will enjoy it, just take the booze out.

If you have a mixer that is ideal, otherwise your wooden spoon is your friend (I have done it both ways many times).

METHOD

1. Preheat your oven to 180°C/160° Fan (350°F) and line a 20cm x 20cm (8-in x 8-in) tray with greaseproof paper.

2. Melt the butter and chocolate gently in a bowl/pan over another pan of boiling water (ensure the pot or bowl isn't touching the water so that the chocolate doesn't burn, which it can do very easily).

3. Take the butter and chocolate off the heat when just melted. Add the sugar, stirring vigorously until thoroughly mixed. Add the eggs, one at a time, mixing in quickly, then add the bourbon. Add the flour and baking powder with a pinch of salt (a little salt enhances the chocolate flavour; remember the bacon has salt too). Mix vigorously for a few minutes until the brownie batter acquires a bit of a sheen and is less grainy. Stir the candied bacon through and pour into the prepared tin.

4. Bake for 25–30 minutes in the oven until the top has just set. Allow to cool. Remove from the tray and cut into 8 slices. Best eaten on the day.

Candied bacon flapjacks

INGREDIENTS

Makes: 12 slices

200g *(7 oz)* butter

100g *(3½ oz)* brown sugar

60ml *(2 fl oz)/* 4 heaped
   tbsp golden syrup

300g *(10½ oz)* porridge
   oats

4 slices *(100g/3½ oz)*
   candied bacon
   (see p.198), chopped into
   small pieces

This idea came from the air. One day, some years ago, I was working on peanut butter and cherry flapjacks (and that recipe will be in my next book!) and I thought to myself, as I did a lot at the time: WHAT IF I PUT BACON IN?! Well, reader, I did, and it was wonderful.

So here you are. Pimp your flapjacks with some candied bacon, and never ever look back.

Confused American readers, I see you! Let me explain. What you call a flapjack, we call a pancake. Our flapjacks are oat bars akin to granola bars for you. Either way, you should make these and embrace our flapjacks.

Yes, it is a lot of butter. Don't worry, butter is good for you!*

*In moderation, as with everything. This is not medical advice, there is only flapjack advice here.

METHOD

1. Preheat your oven to 180°C/160°C Fan (350°F). Line a 20cm x 20cm (8 in x 8 in) baking tray with buttered greaseproof paper.

2. Put the butter, brown sugar and golden syrup into a pan and heat until the butter has melted and the sugar has dissolved. Add the oats and candied bacon and stir through until all of the oats and bacon are coated. Put the flapjack mixture in the tin, smoothing over with a spatula or spoon. Bake for 25 minutes, when the edges will be just browning (but you don't want the centre to brown).

3. Remove from the oven and allow to cool completely. Once cooled a bit, you can speed up the process in the fridge. This makes the flapjacks much easier to slice. Cut into 12 slices and enjoy for breakfast or as a perfect on-the-go or staying-very-still snack. Up to you! These will keep well in an airtight container in the fridge for up to 5 days.

Bacon bourbon eclairs

INGREDIENTS

*Makes approximately
12-14 eclairs*

For the choux pastry:

100g *(3½ oz)* butter

pinch of sea salt

1 tsp brown sugar

250ml *(8½ fl oz)* water

150g *(5½ oz)* flour, sifted
*(strong white if you have
it, but plain flour will
do if not)*

4 eggs, lightly beaten

**For the chocolate
ganache:**

100g *(3½ oz)* butter

100g *(3½ oz)* dark
chocolate *(chopped into
small pieces if it is a bar)*

For the cream filling:

300ml *(10fl oz)* double
cream

1 tbsp maple syrup

25ml *(¾ fl oz)* bourbon

6 slices *(150g/5½ oz)*
maple candied bacon
(see p. 198), chopped

I love eclairs, they were my favourite treat in childhood, along with lemon meringue pies (with a bitter lemon on the side). I still love them. So, it was time for a bacon version of one.

Scarred from my first attempt at making choux pastry from a book in childhood, I attempted again in adulthood and discovered that I had in fact been doing it right before; it is just very different to regular pastry. All of those years of homemade eclairs and cheese gougères denied, but don't feel too sorry for me, I bought plenty and had my fill.

This recipe does sound a little peculiar I know, but it is really tasty, and would make lovely small gougères when you have friends around too.

METHOD

1. Preheat your oven to 200°C/180°C Fan (400°F) and line a baking tray with greaseproof paper.

2. Make your choux pastry. Bring the butter, salt, sugar and water to the boil in a saucepan. When just boiled (don't boil for longer or some of the water will boil off) add the flour in one go, stirring with a wooden spoon as you do.

3. Stir vigorously until the mixture pulls away from the side of the pan. Remove the pan from the heat and let the pastry cool for about 5 minutes, then slowly add the beaten eggs a little at a time, beating them into the pastry as you do. Don't be alarmed if your pastry separates and looks like curds, just keep beating it and bringing it back together. When all of the eggs have been added and the pastry looks glossy and slides gently off the spoon, it is ready.

4. Fill a piping bag with the mixture and pipe out small buns approximately 15cm (6 in) long onto a lined baking tray. If you don't have a piping bag, make small round shapes – like little rough profiteroles – by dropping some of the pastry on to the tray. Ensure they are roughly 2.5cm (1 in) apart.

5. Bake for 10 minutes, then reduce the oven temperature to 180°C/160C Fan (350°F) and bake for a further 10 minutes (they should be a lovely golden brown). Cool the choux buns on a wire rack while you prepare the chocolate ganache and cream.

6. Make the chocolate ganache. Melt the butter in a saucepan, then turn off the heat and add the chocolate in squares and stir until it melts. Let the ganache cool for 10 minutes (only) so that it firms a little but is still glossy and easy to spread.

7. Now for the cream filling. Prepare this just as you finish the ganache and it is cooling. Whip the cream until thick with a whisk (electric or otherwise, electric is of course easiest but not essential). Gently stir in the maple syrup and bourbon. You can mix the chopped bacon through the cream as I did in the photo. Although my preferred way is to sprinkle the bacon on top of the chocolate ganache just after you spread it on the choux buns.

8. When the choux buns have cooled, gently and carefully cut them in half lengthwise with a sharp knife. Fill the choux with the cream, and spread the ganache on top. Now is the time to put the bacon on the ganache. Leave them for about 20 minutes so that the ganache can set, then serve.

Bourbon and bacon ice cream

INGREDIENTS

Makes: approx. 1 litre
(1¼ pints)

600ml *(20fl oz)* full fat milk

1 vanilla bean, spilt in
  half and seeds scraped
  out with a knife *(see
  recommendation for pod,
  above)*

6 large egg yolks

150g *(5½ oz)* soft brown
  sugar

pinch of sea salt

50ml *(2fl oz)* bourbon

250ml *(8¾ fl oz)* single
  cream

6 slices *(150g/5½ oz)*
  maple candied bacon
  (p.184), finely chopped

This ice cream takes a little time but it is absolutely worth it. You will need an ice-cream machine to churn it. If you don't have one already but you love ice cream, you might want to look into it. You can get a relatively inexpensive one that needs the bowl stored in the freezer, or you can splash out on one that is self-contained and will freeze the ice-cream; the latter option is a little bulkier. It really depends on your ice-cream requirements, your budget and your space.

The name of this recipe is the letter 'b' version of rum and raisin ice cream, and this is absolutely intentional. It is a similar concept, but using the dream team of bourbon and candied bacon instead. The first time I made this, many years ago now, it was a very hot day in London. I gave a visiting friend, who had been openly squeamish about my bacon-cooking adventures, a cone with this ice cream. I didn't tell him what was in it. He loved it, very enthusiastically, and was demanding to know what it was. He just couldn't pinpoint it. I waited until he finished before I explained, and he has been asking for it again ever since.

This recipe involves making an egg custard that you must cool before churning, so it takes a bit of time. You can make the custard the day before and churn the ice cream before you need it. Of course, you can also store the finished ice cream in the freezer.

The vanilla pod that is scraped for the seeds in this recipe can also be used for other sweet treats, such as infusing milk for a hot chocolate. You'll need at least a litre of milk, then heat the milk until it is steaming, but don't let it boil. Add the vanilla pod after you have removed the milk from the heat and let it infuse for a couple of hours. Store in the fridge until you need it. You can also blend the vanilla pod with sugar to make vanilla sugar for baking projects.

METHOD

1. Heat the milk in a pan over a medium heat until it starts steaming and has tiny bubbles but isn't boiling. Add the vanilla seeds and stir through, then remove from the heat.

2. In a separate bowl, combine the egg yolks, sugar and sea salt, and whisk until it is thick and pale. Add a ladleful of the warmed milk to the egg mixture, whisking as you do, to introduce the eggs to the idea. This will prevent them curdling when you add them to the pan.

3. Slowly add the egg mixture to the pan of milk, whisking as you do. Return to the heat and cook very slowly over the lowest heat until the liquid reaches pouring consistency: when it becomes a custard that will coat the back of a spoon. Remove from the heat and whisk in the bourbon and cream. Remove to a bowl and let it cool before covering and putting it in the fridge.

4. Leave the mixture in the fridge for an hour or more if you are not planning on churning it yet. When you are ready to churn it, pour the mixture into your ice-cream maker and follow the manufacturer's instructions. When the ice cream is almost ready, add the candied bacon so that it will become well distributed but still hold its form.

Bacon and salted caramel popcorn

INGREDIENTS

For the salted caramel:

200g *(7 oz)* white granulated sugar

100ml *(3½ fl oz)* cold water

100g *(3½ oz)* butter, diced

125ml *(4¼ fl oz)* single cream

1 tsp sea salt

For the popcorn:

50ml *(2fl oz)* neutral oil, like sunflower oil *(or whatever you use at home already)*

100g *(3½ oz)* popcorn kernels

sea salt

50g *(1¾ oz)* butter

6 slices *(125g/4½ oz)* maple candied bacon, chopped small *(see p.198)*

Popcorn is an easy, speedy and satisfying treat. There are many ways of making it very tasty, as popcorn does need a little help there. Lots of butter! Always a good start. Grated Parmesan cheese and freshly ground black pepper? Yes! Let's ramp it up another gear and top our popcorn with salted caramel and candied bacon. I have your attention now, I bet. Uh huh. Friday nights will never be the same again. Any night!

Popcorn seems easy but I have another story about the first time I made it and it was a disaster. In my defence, I was a child making it up as I went, suffice to say there was yellow smoke and the pot was destroyed. You may already be a high-grade popcorn chef (add that to your CV!) but just in case you are not, I will take you through it in detail.

METHOD

1. Let's start with the salted caramel. You can make caramel without a thermometer; trust your eyes and nose and you will be fine. I make a wet caramel with water, as I find it best for a sauce and it is also easier to make. Put the sugar and water in a heavy-bottomed pan over a medium heat. You want to make sure the sugar is covered, so add more water if you need to.

2. You can stir the sugar and water until the sugar is melted, after that just swirl the pan to dissolve any sugar crystals at the side. If you stir it further you may encourage clumping and get a gritty caramel. The sugar will start to become golden as the sugar caramelises, you are looking for a deep amber colour (it will smell like caramel too). Turn off the heat immediately and remove the pan from the hob/stovetop and any residual heat there.

3. Add the butter, cream and salt and whisk in quickly and carefully (it is HOT!). The caramel will bubble furiously, but don't worry about that. Work quickly, as the butter and cream will reduce the caramel temperature very quickly. Leave on the side while we prepare our popcorn.

4. Popcorn time and almost time to eat! Heat the oil in a large heavy-bottomed pan with a tight-fitting lid over a medium-high heat. Put a few popcorn kernels in there. They will act like our little popcorn canaries in the mine. As soon as you hear those few start to pop, remove the lid and add the remaining popcorn. Put the lid on, and give the pan a good shake to ensure the popcorn kernels all get a slick of oil. Once the popcorn starts popping earnestly (about a minute later) give the pan a good shake again. When the popping starts to slow down, take the pan off the heat. Give it a minute, then empty the popcorn into a bowl and salt it with some sea salt.

5. The pan should be empty but remove any popcorn that might have clung on. Add the butter to the pan. It will melt in the residual heat. Pour the butter over the popcorn and mix well with a spoon.

6. I like to serve this on a platter so there is plenty of bacon and salted caramel. A bowl works well too, of course! Add the candied bacon to the popcorn and mix well. Finish with the salted caramel sauce and dig in. If you don't finish all your salted caramel (unlikely!) you can store it covered in the fridge for up to 2 weeks. Before using, heat it gently over a pan of boiling water until it has loosened, stirring occasionally (about 5 minutes).

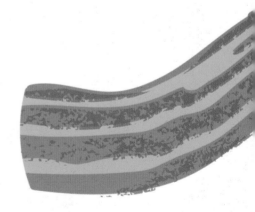

Boozy bacon chocolate truffles

INGREDIENTS

*Makes: approx.
16–20 truffles*

200ml *(7fl oz)* single cream

200g *(7 oz)* dark
chocolate, chopped
small if it is a bar

25ml *(1fl oz)* whiskey, rum
or bourbon *(your choice)*

4 slices *(100g / 3½ oz)*
maple candied bacon,
chopped finely *(see
p.198)*

50g *(1¼ oz)* cocoa

Chocolate truffles are easy, tasty and fun. There are no complications here and no thermometers. These truffles also come together quickly.

If making these truffles for a family occasion or kiddies, leave out the booze and replace it with 25ml (1fl oz) cream.

METHOD

1. Heat the cream gently in a saucepan until it just shivers (if you boil it, the taste will change and it will be too hot for the chocolate). Remove the pan from the heat and add the chocolate, stirring in to melt. When fully melted and glossy, add the booze and candied bacon. Stir in well and then decant into a shallow dish and leave to chill in the fridge for 2 hours until firm.

2. Put the cocoa on a plate and scoop your truffles out from the dish with a teaspoon or, for a near-perfect round truffle, with a melon baller. I like them to be rough and ready, as a bacon truffle would demand. Roll the truffles in the cocoa and they are ready to serve. These will keep in an airtight container in the fridge for up to 1 week.

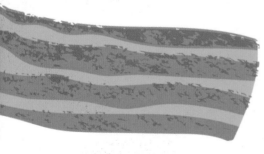

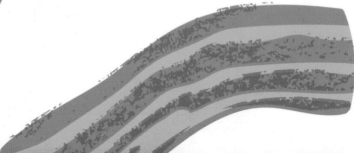

Bacon chocolate bark with almonds and sour cherries

INGREDIENTS

Serves: 1

100g *(3½ oz)* chocolate of
  your choice – I like dark
  chocolate

2 tbsp blanched almonds

2 slices *(50g/1¼ oz)*
  maple candied bacon,
  chopped small *(see
  p.198)*

2 tbsp dried cherries
  *(dried cranberries work
  well here also)*

This is one of the flexible and easy recipes in this chapter. It comes together quickly and looks and tastes great, making candied bacon chocolate bark the perfect last-minute gift for the bacon fiend in your life. It is also the perfect thing for you when you have had a day that demands it.

This recipe makes one portion, and I use a 450g (1lb) loaf tin lined with greaseproof paper to shape it. It is the size of a standard large chocolate bar, but it is studded with goodies. Feel free to shape it in whatever vessel you like; you can make smaller-sized bacon barks too and serve them that way on social occasions. Expand the quantities relative to how much you want and need.

Again, I don't worry about tempering the chocolate here. This is about home cooking and getting the best results without too much unnecessary effort.

METHOD

1. Prepare your loaf tin, or whatever you are using to shape your bark, by lining it with greaseproof paper.

2. Melt your chocolate in a bowl that fits over a pan of boiling water. The bowl should not touch the water. Chop your chocolate into roughly even sizes, so that they all melt together. When the chocolate has melted completely, remove it from the heat. Don't leave it sitting on the boiling water too long as you might scorch the chocolate. Chocolate melts at human body temperature, hence the term 'melt in the mouth'.

3. While your chocolate is melting, toast your almonds until golden in a dry frying pan. Shake the pan while they are toasting so

that they brown evenly. It will take just a few minutes. Remove the almonds from the pan as soon as they are ready, to stop them cooking in the residual heat.

4. Pour the melted chocolate into your greaseproof-lined tin. Immediately stud it with the toasted almonds, bacon and sour cherries and allow to cool. Once cold, it is ready to eat. You can store it in an airtight container in the fridge for up to 5 days.

Candied bacon chocolate chip cookies

INGREDIENTS

Makes 12 cookies

125g *(4½ oz)* butter, at room temperature *(remove it from the fridge 2 hours before)*

100g *(3½ oz)* demerara sugar

50g *(1¾ oz)* white granulated sugar

1 egg

¼ tsp fine sea salt

180g *(6 ⊠ oz)* plain flour

½ tsp bicarbonate of soda

100g *(3½ oz)* dark chocolate, cut into chunks

3 slices *(75g / 2¼ oz)* candied bacon *(see p.198)*, cut into small pieces

This cookie recipe is a cookie recipe that works, pure and simple. It is low on drama and high on taste. Chocolate chips mingle with bits of candied bacon.

There is always a lot of mystery and conflicting tips around cookies. When you look at the details, you can see the little things that you need to pay attention to in order to get good results.

Chill your dough – Cookie dough that is chilled before baking produces better-shaped and better-tasting, puffier cookies. This is because the chilled fats melt more slowly while baking, and the cookies won't spread as much as they would if they were at room temperature. Cookie dough that is at room temperature before baking will spread and flatten out in the warm oven.

How long should you chill your cookie dough for? Cookie dough that is chilled overnight will have better flavour as well as texture. This is because the flour has time to fully hydrate, which can be a slow process when the main fluid is eggs. Refrigerating at least overnight (some recommend 72 hours) is fine here, and by doing this, we will ensure that we get cookies that bake more evenly and have better flavour.

Niche fact: chilling cookie dough is called ripening.

Use greaseproof paper – Greaseproof paper will ensure your cookies retain a good shape. If you put the dough directly on a buttered tray, you run the risk of the cookies spreading out, and if you don't grease the tray, they will likely stick.

Use a cookie scoop – A cookie scoop will ensure even more consistent results. If you bake a lot of cookies, it is a worthwhile investment. A cookie scoop is like a small ice-cream scoop (you can use a small ice cream scoop in its place), and I wouldn't suggest you get one especially unless you make a lot of cookies. (But if you do, you should!) If you have neither of these things, and that is fine, you can roll the dough into evenly sized balls before baking.

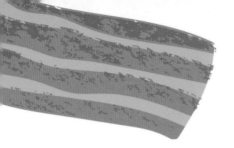

But bear in mind that your hands are warm, so do this quickly, and if you have time, stick the dough balls back in the fridge for a bit before baking.

Choosing your sugar – I use 2 parts demerara to 1 part white granulated sugar here. This demerara adds a little moisture to the cookie dough, ensuring a softer cookie. White sugar results in a flatter, crisper cookie.

METHOD

1. Cream the butter and sugar together until light and fluffy. The colour will be lighter and it will have increased in size because you have introduced air. This air allows the raising agent to get to work. You can do this with a mixer but also by hand with a wooden spoon. It will take a while by hand but it is a key step, so persevere and know that it will be worth it.

2. Beat in the egg, then add the remaining ingredients (just a little salt as the bacon is salty). It is important not to overmix at this stage or you will aerate the dough too much and get flat, crisp cookies, which is not what we want. But don't undermix either. As soon as you can see that the wet and dry ingredients are well combined, you can stop. Chill the dough overnight if you can, or at least for an hour.

3. When you are ready to bake the cookies, preheat your oven to 180°C /160°C Fan (350°F).

4. Line two flat baking sheets with greaseproof paper. Divide the dough into 12 balls using a cookie or ice cream scoop, or shape the balls quickly using your hands (see recipe introduction for more details). Place 6 dough balls on each sheet, leaving as much space as you can between each cookie. Bake for 12 minutes, when the edges will be firm and the centres still soft. Cool on a wire rack and store in an airtight container. Best eaten on the day.

Bacon peanut brittle

INGREDIENTS

Serves: approx. 6
  (to share)

fine sea salt

150g *(5½ oz)* blanched
  peanuts

180g *(6⅓ oz)* granulated
  white sugar

200ml *(7fl oz)* golden
  syrup

75g *(2¼ oz)* butter

4 slices *(100g / 3½ oz)*
  maple candied bacon
  (see p.198), chopped
  small

We are getting our thermometers out again for this one. Precision is important here, as we want to ensure the sugars reach the 'hard crack' stages like toffee, so that we get that perfect snap.

I like to use blanched peanuts and toast them to my liking at home. If you prefer or want to save time, you can use roasted peanuts.

Another perfect gift, another perfect snack for you.

METHOD

1. Preheat the oven to 180°C / 160°C Fan (350°F). Salt your peanuts and roast them in a single layer on a greaseproof-lined oven tray for 10 minutes until golden but not brown. Remove from the oven and leave to cool. You can use this tray and greaseproof paper for the bark itself also.

2. Put the sugar, golden syrup and butter in a saucepan over a medium heat. Stir and keep a very close eye, checking the temperature intermittently, until the mixture reaches 150°C (and no more). Remove from the heat immediately and stir in the peanuts first and then the candied bacon.

3. Transfer the mixture to the waiting tray lined with greaseproof paper and spread it out with a spatula. Allow to cool. Enjoy best on the day. Refrigerating peanut brittle is not recommended, as the moisture will make the brittle soggy, and no one wants that.

Candied bacon maple lollipops

INGREDIENTS

Makes: 8 lollipops

250ml *(8½ fl oz)*
   maple syrup

8 lollipop sticks

2 slices *(50g / 1¼ oz)*
   maple candied bacon
   (see p.198), chopped
   small

These are ridiculously simple and could not be easier. It was a bit of fun one day that demanded inclusion in this book. You do need a thermometer here again

You might be wondering where to get lollipop sticks. I sourced mine online with ease. A fun project and when you have lots of lollipop sticks, you can make lots of lollipops.

METHOD

1. Line an oven tray with greaseproof paper.

2. Heat the maple syrup in a pan over a medium heat, keeping a very close eye on it until it is 150°C (and no higher).

3. Pour the maple syrup – very carefully, it is very very hot! – on to the tray lined with greaseproof paper. You're aiming for 8 lollipop shapes with the liquid, but let them shape as they land, like irregular amber puddles. Put a lollipop stick in each shape, making sure that the stick reaches at least 1cm (one-third of an inch) inside. Sprinkle the candied bacon on and allow to cool. Best made to be eaten on the day, as even if they are well-wrapped in an airtight container, you run the risk of them going soggy.

Candied bacon marshmallows

INGREDIENTS

Makes approximately 30 chunky marshmallows

16–17g *(0.56–0.6 oz)* leaf gelatine *(approx, as above)*

550ml *(18½ fl oz)* water

200g *(7 oz)* granulated white sugar

100ml *(3½ fl oz)* golden syrup

4 large egg whites

1 tsp vanilla extract

4 slices *(100g/3½ oz)* maple candied bacon *(p.198)*, chopped as fine as you can

100g *(3½ oz)* icing sugar

40g *(1½ oz)* cornflour

These are divisive, but I find the best things often are. Homemade marshmallow is a complete treat, anyway. It seems complex but when you understand what is going on, it is easy.

It is simple: the egg white provides the fluff, the sugars heated to firm-ball stage (118°C–120°C) provide the structure, and the gelatine provides the wobble.

Marshmallows from scratch are another recipe from my cooking classes; this time not a bacon class but in a confectionery class that I designed and was teaching for a while. It was a lot of fun!

I use gelatine to set my marshmallows, and if you are amenable to putting bacon in your marshmallows, I don't need to offer gelatine alternatives, right?

One thing I will recommend is choosing gelatine sheets over powder for this recipe, as I developed my recipes with sheets. I prefer using them. Confusingly, there are different grades of gelatine and different brands have sheets with different weights. With a little maths we can figure out what you need, so let's get that phone calculator out.

My local supermarket sells a pack of 8 gelatine leaves that weighs 13g (0.46 oz) in total, so I calculate the weight per sheet (1.63g/0.05oz). 10 sheets will get us to 16.3g (0.57 oz). Once you are between 16–17g gelatine (0.56–0.6 oz), your marshmallow will be good.

You will need a thermometer.

METHOD

1. Soak the gelatine leaves in 450ml (15¼ fl oz) of the cold water.

2. Combine the sugar, golden syrup and the remaining 100ml (3½ fl oz) water in a pan and bring to 118°C–120°C (no higher) over a medium to high heat. Use your thermometer to check the temperatur

3. While the sugar and golden syrup are coming to temperature, whisk the egg whites at low speed (a mixer or electric whisk will make your life a lot easier, as we pick up the pace). When the sugar syrup is almost at temperature, turn up the mixer to high and whisk the egg whites until fluffy and in soft peaks. It is important not to do this in advance. Once the sugars have reached temperature, carefully add them in a slow steady stream to the egg white while the mixer is still running. Then add the vanilla extract.

4. Remove the soaked gelatine leaves from the water and give them a good squeeze. Put them in the saucepan you just used to heat the sugars, where they will melt in the residual heat. Pour the liquid gelatine into the egg whites while the mixer is still running and let it continue to run until the mixer bowl of marshmallow is cool to touch.

5. You can go two ways with your bacon, you can add it to the icing sugar and cornflour mix by blending them with the candied bacon until as fine as you can get it. Or you can add it to the marshmallow itself. I used to do it the second way but now I prefer the first texturally, with the bacon on the outside like a very tasty protector of the realm.

6. After mixing the icing sugar and cornflour together, use a sieve to sprinkle it over a waiting baking tray lined with greaseproof paper, ensuring the bottom and sides are well dusted. Pour your marshmallow mix into the tin, spreading it evenly with a spatula. Sprinkle more of the icing sugar and cornflour mix on top.

7. Leave to set for 4 hours uncovered and cut the next day with a sharp knife dusted with the icing sugar and cornflour mix. Toss the cut marshmallow pieces in the icing sugar and cornflour mix. When serving, shake them slightly to remove any excess powder. Generally, you would store marshmallows in an airtight container at room temperature. These have bacon in, so it is best to store them in an airtight container in the fridge, with extra cornstarch and icing sugar to stop them getting sticky. They will keep for up to 5 days.

Bacon Krispie marshmallow bars

INGREDIENTS

Makes 8 bars

50g *(1¾ oz)* butter

220g *(7¾ oz)* marshmallows

150g *(5½ oz)* Rice Krispies *(Rice Bubbles, for the Australians/New Zealanders)*

3 slices *(75g/ 2¼ oz)* finely chopped candied bacon *(p.198)*

These became a regular treat for a long time after I first made them. I still love them and make them often. They are like the marshmallow Rice Krispie bars of your childhood, but they have candied bacon in. Of course, if you live in Australia or New Zealand, you get to call your Rice Krispies 'Rice Bubbles', how fun is that?!

I generally use regular store-bought marshmallows for these.

Yes, that is right, they do look good. Run right to the kitchen! I am running to mine, bag of marshmallows in hand.

METHOD

1. Melt the butter in a pan over a low heat and add the marshmallows. They will melt quite quickly. Take off the heat and add the Rice Krispies and bacon and stir through.

2. Decant the mixture to a greaseproof-lined baking tin and smooth out with a spatula so that it is even. Leave to cool, and when cold, slice into 8 bars.

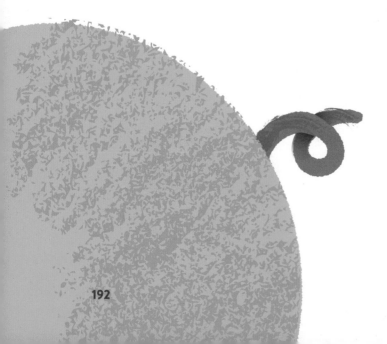

Bacon Pantry

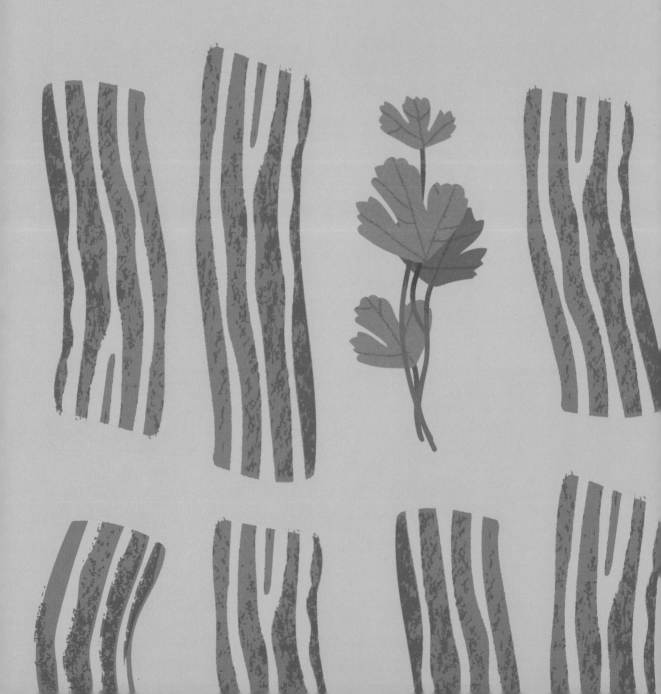

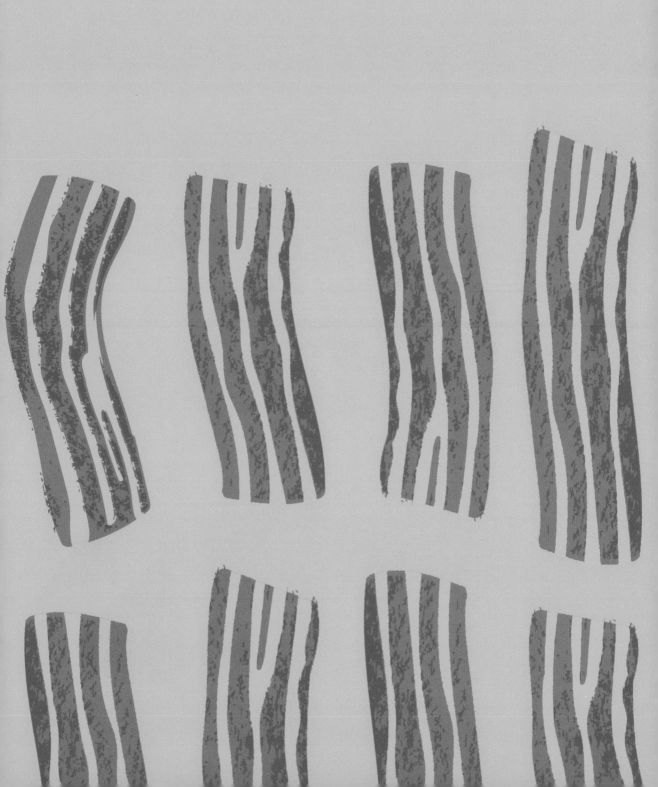

Bacon Pantry

Building even a small pantry of homemade products is a great way of extending your favourite flavours that are blended expertly for your palate throughout your food. Homemade is almost always better too.

This chapter could also have been called Bacon Instant Gratification, because that is exactly what it is. Not that you make these recipes in an instant, but that you set up your future self with lots of instant bacon possibilities.

I love to have sauces and condiments on hand to add instant flavour to something simple, mostly when I am too tired or time-strapped to properly cook. Cheese Sandwich? Ok. Bacon Jam Cheese Sandwich? OK!

Put Candied Bacon Salt on your eggs and never ever ever, and I mean EVER, look back. Candy all the bacon you can find too, in multiple ways, and try not to eat it all on the day you make it.

Scroll through and start planning. You are going to make butters and sauces and jams and condiments that will up your eating game.

I always say that anyone aspiring to meet someone and persuade them that they are 'the one', at least for now, should always carry a small jar of their homemade bacon jam around with them. Disclaimer: I don't, but you should. A little bag of candied bacon fudge too.

Candied Bacon

How to open the Pantry chapter? With one of the easiest and most satisfying bites of all, and the most used ingredient in this book. Candied bacon!

You can candy bacon in many ways. Sugar meets bacon meets heat gives candied bacon.

That is maths, I don't know if you noticed that. I thought I might sneak an equation in:

Sugar + bacon + heat = Satisfaction + JOY

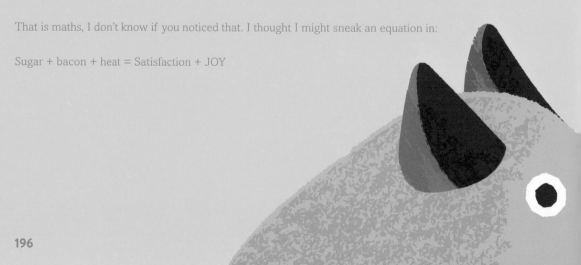

Sugar comes in many guises. White granulated sugar is essential for confectionery because it doesn't have much moisture, the molasses has been removed, and so it behaves exactly as expected. White sugar will transform in specific ways at specific temperatures to make different types of sweets.

Brown sugar still has some molasses and has more moisture (you can feel this when you touch it). Brown sugar has more flavour, and where flavour is important I use it. Brown sugar doesn't burn as quickly as white sugar does, so it makes terrific marinades and rubs. White sugar doesn't bring flavour, it brings sweetness. With confectionery, white sugar provides the structure and sweetness but the flavour comes from elsewhere (like butter in butter toffee, caramelised milk sugars in fudge).

Maple syrup and honey are also sugars: sugars in a fur coat with designer sunglasses. Palm sugar is made from the nectar of coconut blossom, which is first reduced to a syrup and then boiled down to sugar. All make excellent candied bacon. If it's sugar and it meets bacon with heat in a controlled way, you have got yourself something fabulous.

Start with a classic simple candied bacon like Maple Syrup Candied Bacon or Brown Sugar Candied Bacon. We roast it until the sugar hits a temperature in which it turns to toffee but, combined with bacon fat, clings to its strip of bacon (recipe follows). You can also do this under the grill (remember to turn it carefully with a pair of tongs) and even on the hob/stovetop. I have fried lardons until golden brown, added sugar and cooked it until candied too and it works very well.

Do not leave that sugar or leftover maple syrup behind, sad and neglected on an oven tray. That candied bacon detritus is bacon fat and caramel, and that is (yet more) liquid gold. You might have thin shards of toffee there too. When I was serving candied bacon every day for 6 weeks at a pop-up, I stored that amber path to joy in a jar for future use. (You can fat-wash spirits such as vodka, whiskey, rum, etc. with candied bacon to make cocktails – see Bacon Bloody Mary, p.50).

How thick should your bacon be? Some people prefer to candy bacon that is thinly sliced. I like thicker-sliced candied bacon too. I like to get the taste and texture of a quality, dry-cured streaky bacon underneath my candy. Sometimes I might want curls of thin-sliced candied bacon, which are more sugar than meat. These make a great garnish too.

The only thing to note is that if you are going to candy bacon that is thinly sliced it will have a shorter cooking time, and it will also have a tendency to curl up. Maybe you want that, but if you don't, put another layer of greaseproof paper on top of the bacon and sugar of your choice, and press another baking tray on top of it so that as it candies it will keep it flat.

Maple candied bacon

INGREDIENTS

Makes: 12 slices

12 slices smoked streaky
  bacon
100ml *(3½ fl oz)* maple
  syrup

I start with maple syrup candied bacon because it is the one
I use most often. I adore the flavour and it is a bit of a treat.

If you have arrived here because you need candied bacon for
another recipe in this book, you can assume, roughly, that each
slice of candied bacon is 20g–25g (¾oz–1 oz), depending on how
thick your bacon is. Precision isn't absolutely necessary here

To make a brown sugar version, use 1 tablespoon of brown sugar on
each slice of bacon (a half-tablespoon pressed firmly on either side).
I wouldn't use dark brown sugar for this, use demerara or soft brown
sugar for better results.

METHOD

1. Preheat your oven to 180°C/160°C Fan (350°F).

2. Put the bacon and maple syrup in a bowl and massage together,
making sure they get to know each other very well. If you have time,
let them sit together in the fridge for an hour (ensure the bowl is
covered).

3. Line a large baking tray with greaseproof paper. Lay the bacon
strips out flat in a row. Pour the maple syrup that remains in the
bowl over the bacon.

4. Bake for 10 minutes. Remove from the oven and very carefully
turn each bacon slice with a pair of tongs. Put back in the oven for
another 10 minutes and check it. When you lift the bacon with tongs,
you should see little amber strings clinging on. If it is not there yet,
put it back in the oven and keep an eye on it. It won't take much
longer.

5. Leave to cool once it is done. It will be very hot, so resist any
urge to taste it until it has cooled a bit. It stores well in the fridge
wrapped with greaseproof paper in an airtight container for
5 days.

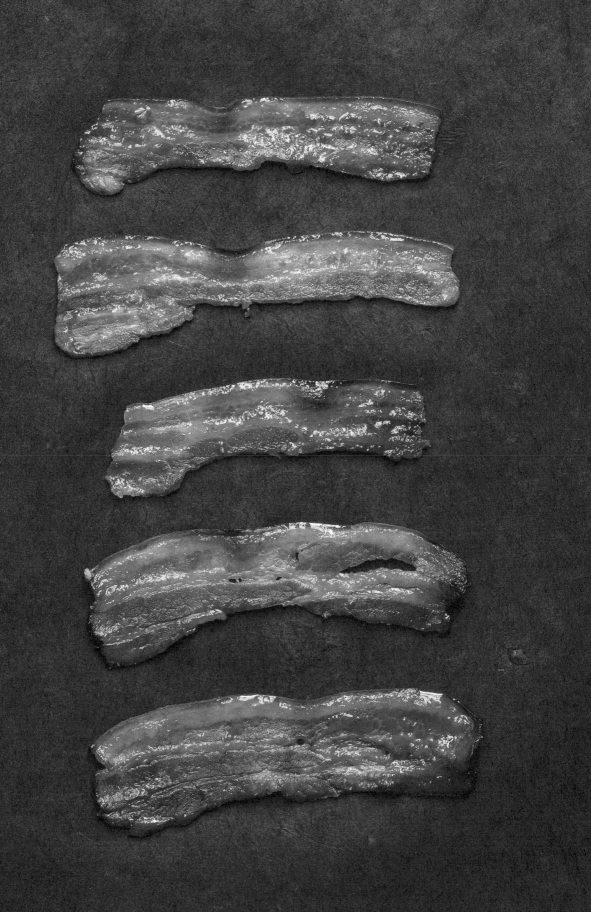

Maple, chilli and tamarind candied bacon

INGREDIENTS

Makes: 12 slices

½ tsp of tamarind
concentrate

1 tsp chilli flakes *(I like
to use pasilla, chipotle
or Korean gochugaru,
which is a bit milder)*

100ml *(3½ fl oz)* maple
syrup

12 slices smoked
streaky bacon

METHOD

Now we have our sweet bacon, we can think about how we can
enhance those flavours and make them even better.

Sure, and back to the maths:

Bacon + sugar = Magic

But, what if you added something tangy in there and something hot?
Oh woah, you see where I am going here.

Tamarind is a wonderful ingredient. It brings sourness, a slight
sweetness and depth while retaining some brightness, even a hint of
citrus. It doesn't just enhance other flavours, it brings its own while
doing so, but in a friendly, let's be friends way.

Tamarind is a legume, and you can buy it as it grows: in a pod.
The pulp around the seeds within is what we love. You can buy
pressed tamarind too – in a block, or you can buy a paste or a
concentrate. For our purposes we ideally want tamarind concentrate,
but we can work with paste. We want the flavour but not too much
moisture, as moisture will interfere with the candying process.

You can source tamarind easily online and in Indian and Asian
food shops. My local supermarket sells it also.

METHOD

1. Preheat your oven to 180°C/160°C Fan (350°F).

2. Combine the tamarind, chilli and maple syrup in a large bowl
and mix well. Then follow the Maple Candied Bacon recipe
(p.198) exactly.

Espresso and brown sugar candied bacon

INGREDIENTS

Makes: 12 slices

150g *(5½ oz)* demerara
or soft brown sugar

50ml *(2fl oz)* espresso
coffee or fresh
strong coffee

12 slices smoked
streaky bacon

METHOD

1. Preheat your oven to 180°C/160°C Fan (350°F).

2. Combine the sugar and espresso or coffee and mix well. Lay your bacon out on a large baking tray lined with greaseproof paper. Pat the sugar-coffee mix on to each slice of bacon firmly. Turn the slices over and repeat.

3. Bake as for the Maple Candied Bacon (p.198), for 10 minutes on each side, turning very carefully after 10 minutes and removing from the oven when the sugar is golden and you see sugar strings forming when you pull a slice of bacon with a pair of tongs.

4. Leave to cool before eating. Stores in the fridge for up to 5 days wrapped with greaseproof paper in an airtight container.

Candied bacon salt

INGREDIENTS

*Makes: 300g (10½ oz)
candied bacon salt*

50g *(1¾ oz)* candied
bacon (see p. 198)

250g *(9 oz)* sea salt

But, what will I do with all that candied bacon? Firstly, I am surprised that you have any left. More power to your willpower. Secondly, if you (like me) ate it all or used it for other recipes, make extra next time and absolutely make this salt.

Candied bacon salt is punchy. It is a game changer for cocktails: line the rim of a bacon-friendly or bacon-containing drink with this salt. Sprinkle it on your eggs, it's too good. You can add chilli to this too to make it more of a seasoning.

METHOD

1. Coarsely chop your bacon first, then add it to your blender or food processor with half the salt and blend until fine. Add the remaining salt and blend until it is fine but still has some texture. Store in an airtight container in the fridge for up to a week.

Bacon jam: classic

INGREDIENTS

*Makes: approx. 2 x 370ml
(12½ fl oz) jars*

500g *(1lb, 2oz)* smoked
streaky bacon,
finely sliced

1 red onion, peeled and
finely chopped

3 cloves garlic, peeled
and finely chopped

50g *(1¾ oz)* brown sugar

50ml *(2fl oz)* maple syrup

50ml *(2fl oz)* cider vinegar

250ml *(8¾ fl oz)* freshly
brewed coffee

The idea of bacon jam is perplexing, although unless this is the first recipe you have read in this book, and especially if you have yet to explore the Bacon is Sweet chapter, you won't find it surprising at all.

When you think of jam, you think of sweet fruit preserves. This is more of a chutney, but we call it jam. I didn't invent it and I didn't make the rules.

The base of all good bacon jams is bacon and onion, sugar and vinegar. Bacon, because bacon, and onion because not only is it a friend to bacon, it brings sweetness and texture too. Sugar and vinegar bring sweet and sour.

You can add many other things. It is common to include coffee and I include it in this classic bacon jam too.

In terms of storage, if you have jam jars that you can recycle, this is a great option. Just use as many jars as you need, and make sure you sterilise them first so that they are food-safe. You can do this by washing them in a high-temperature wash in the dishwasher. You can also sterilise the jars in the oven. Wash them in hot soapy water and rinse, but don't dry them. Put them on a clean oven tray, open side up, at 160°C (320°F) for 15 minutes with their lids also on the tray (if they are metal). Make sure your hands are freshly washed when you handle them afterwards.

METHOD

1. Sauté the bacon over a medium heat in a wide pot until starting to crisp and the fat starts to render out. Remove the bacon to a plate on the side.

2. Fry the onion in the rendered bacon fat until starting to soften, about 8 minutes. Add the garlic and stir for a minute. Add the fried bacon to the onion and garlic with the remaining ingredients. Bring to the boil and reduce the heat to low.

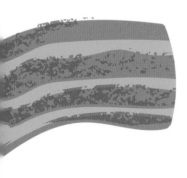

3. Don't put a lid on the pan. Let it cook gently, stirring occasionally. The sugars will caramelise, so you want to make sure they don't catch the bacon at the base of the pan and burn. If it looks like it is getting dry, add a little boiling water from the kettle, and continue to do this until you don't need to anymore because you have a very tasty, shiny bacon jam.

4. At this point you may want to blend the jam or you may want to keep it as it is. That is entirely up to you. Blending it is useful for the Scallops, Bacon Jam and Tomato recipe (p.102) but it loses its gloss. I like to serve bacon jam with cheesy potato skins, sour cream and chives too. This keeps well in the fridge in an airtight container for up to a week (but it's so divine it will disappear well before then).

Chipotle bacon jam

Proceed as per the classic Bacon Jam (p.202), but add 3 chipotles in adobo, including some of the sauce. Add with the coffee (you can purée them with the coffee or chop them small). You can substitute other favourite chillies and flavours too. Some of my favourites follow.

Stout and treacle bacon jam

INGREDIENTS

500g *(1lb, 2oz)* smoked streaky bacon, finely sliced

2 red onions, peeled and finely chopped

3 cloves garlic, peeled and finely chopped

50g *(2¼ oz)* treacle

50ml *(2fl oz)* cider vinegar

250ml *(8¾ fl oz)* stout

METHOD

Proceed as per classic Bacon Jam recipe (p.202), but with these ingredients.

As the recipe is nearing the end, taste and adjust the treacle and/or cider vinegar according to your taste.

Gochujang and cider bacon jam

INGREDIENTS

500g *(1lb, 2oz)* smoked streaky bacon, finely sliced

1 red onion, peeled and finely chopped

3 cloves garlic, peeled and finely chopped

1 thumb-sized piece of ginger, peeled and finely chopped

50ml *(2fl oz)* honey

50ml *(2fl oz)* cider vinegar

2 tbsp gochujang

250ml *(8¾ fl oz)* cider

Gochujang is one of my absolute favourite ingredients. An umami-packed fermented red pepper paste from Korea, it adds instant character and interest to everything that it is used in. Gojuchang is a shortcut to flavour and satisfaction and it goes with everything. Everything yes, but it is a special friend to bacon.

I combine it with cider here. Cider being a favourite drink; the subtle apple flavour and acidity go very well with both the gochujang and bacon.

METHOD

Proceed as per classic Bacon Jam (p.202), but with these ingredients. Add the ginger with the garlic, and add the gochujang, cider vinegar and honey at the same time.

Bacon maple butter

INGREDIENTS

Makes: 375g (13oz)

250g *(9 oz)* butter, at room temperature

125ml *(4¼ fl oz)* maple syrup

50g *(1¾ oz)* maple candied bacon *(p.198)*, chopped very small

Over many trips to Canada, I developed an obsession with maple butter, and would always bring lots home. Particularly on the occasions when I visited Quebec where you can buy it in gorgeous tins, which I love to have in my kitchen. I use them up very fast, I adore the stuff.

Maple butter is another thing that I encountered there in two ways. The first being maple 'butter', which has no actual butter in it at all (much like apple butter). Maple butter is a confection of maple syrup. It is pure maple syrup that is heated to 112°C (237°F) and then whipped (much like fudge). It is delicious and perfect with bacon.

The second maple butter is the one I am sharing here: maple syrup whipped with softened butter. I found that the best ratio is 2 parts butter to 1 part syrup. I serve it with a generous sprinkle of candied bacon. It is gorgeous.

METHOD

1. Making the maple butter itself is fast and easiest done in a mixer or with an electric mix. Just beat all the ingredients together until they are fluffy. Done!

2. To serve, place all the maple butter in a bowl, or big dollops of individual servings on plates or in ramekins, generously sprinkled with the candied bacon.

Bacon peanut butter

INGREDIENTS

Makes: 1 x 370ml (12½ fl oz) jar

200g *(7 oz)* blanched peanuts

50g *(1¾ oz)* candied bacon *(p.198)*

50ml *(2fl oz)* groundnut or peanut oil

50ml *(2fl oz)* maple syrup

1 tsp sea salt

You either know to trust me now or you don't need me to tell you how good this is.

METHOD

1. Preheat your oven to 180°C/160°C fan (350°F).

2. Spread the peanuts on a single layer over two trays and roast until golden, about 10 minutes.

3. Remove from the oven and allow to cool. Blend to a paste. This will take about 5 minutes, depending on your blender. It is best to do this in a high-powered blender, which I have now, but I did use just a cheap stick blender for many years. If using a regular blender, you may struggle to get a paste, and if that is the case, add a little more oil, but not too much.

4. Add the remaining ingredients (and just half the salt) and blend. Check the taste, and if you feel it needs more salt, add the rest in. The saltiness of bacon varies, so it is wise to check

Bacon mayonnaise

INGREDIENTS

Makes: approx. 300ml (10fl oz)

120ml *(4fl oz)* clarified bacon fat

2 large egg yolks

1 tbsp mustard *(I like Dijon but if you want some heat, use English mustard)*

1 tbsp freshly squeezed lemon juice

120ml *(4fl oz)* neutral oil *(like sunflower oil)*

sea salt, to taste

So, you have been hoarding your bacon drippings in the fridge for a while, and you love cooking with it, but what else can you do? You can make gorgeous bacon mayonnaise. Homemade mayonnaise is so luxurious, even though it is made from a list of simple everyday ingredients (it really is amazing what you can do with an egg). Add bacon to the mix and it is a treasure.

You do need to clarify your bacon fat first. This simply means removing the impurities from the fat so that you only have pure bacon fat left. To do this, you need to boil your bacon fat with the same amount of water. Then remove from the heat and transfer to a cold container. Add the same amount of water as fat again, this time cold, and refrigerate for a few hours until the fat separates and rises to the top. Remove the clarified fat and discard the water.

METHOD

1. Heat the bacon fat until liquid but not hot.

2. Combine the egg yolks, mustard and half the lemon juice in your blender and blend until smooth. Or use an electric whisk.

3. Add the oil in a very slow stream, starting with just drops, so as not to split the egg. As the mixture becomes thick and creamy and looks like mayonnaise, you can speed up a little. When the oil is all incorporated, add the liquid bacon fat in a slow, steady stream. Add some salt, and taste to check both the salt and lemon level. Add more of the lemon juice if it needs it, and the salt.

Bacon chipotle ketchup

INGREDIENTS

*Makes: approx. 1 litre
    (1¾ pints)*

300g *(10½ oz)* smoked
    streaky bacon,
    finely sliced

1 red onion, finely diced

3 cloves garlic, peeled and
    finely chopped

2 x 400g *(14 oz)* tins
    tomatoes

5 chipotles in adobo

50ml *(2fl oz)* cider vinegar

50g *(1¾ oz)* soft
    brown sugar

salt, to taste

This is a lovely thing to have. So much flavour. Perfect on burgers, on a bacon or cheese sandwich, with chips, and wherever you have your ketchup.

It is quite punchy in its heat, so dial it down if that is too much for you. If you can't get chipotles in adobo feel free to substitute other chillies. Pickled jalapenos would go very well in here. They are milder so you might need more.

METHOD

1. Fry your bacon in its own fat first over a medium heat, or with a little oil if it doesn't have enough fat. When it is golden brown and has rendered much of its fat, add the red onion and reduce the heat to low. Cook for 8 minutes, stirring occasionally (onions need time and you will be thankful you gave it to them). Add the garlic for a minute further, then add the rest of the ingredients.

2. Cook over a low heat for 30 minutes. Taste and season and adjust sweetness, vinegar or salt if required. Blend and store in the fridge for up to a week.

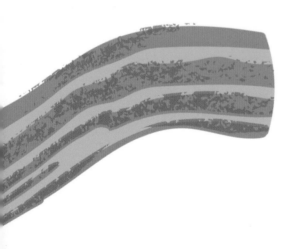

Bacon hot sauce

INGREDIENTS

Makes: approx. 600ml
(1 pint)

300g *(10½ oz)* smoked
   streaky bacon, finely
   sliced

3 scotch bonnets

6 cayenne chillies

25g *(1 oz)* gochugaru

300ml *(10fl oz)* cider
   vinegar

25ml *(1fl oz)* maple syrup
   or honey

2 red onions, peeled and
   coarsely chopped

4 cloves garlic, peeled
   and coarsely chopped

5g fine sea salt

I love naturally fermented hot sauces and have made these myself at home. With bacon I keep it simpler, out of necessity, but also simple is good and it works well. Use fresh chillies rather than dried, as you want their fruitiness.

This chili sauce is not a melter. It has gorgeous round flavour, and it is hot, but it is totally manageable. I only use 9 fresh chillies here, of two varieties (feel free to mix it up). The jewel in the crown is gochugaru, Korean red pepper flakes which are gently hot and also fruity. They give this sauce a lovely red colour too.

I make this sauce quite thick to dollop on my eggs. You can thin it out by adding more cider vinegar, which you may want to balance out with a little maple syrup. I like to store this in flip-top preserver bottles. Use any bottle you like, just make sure you sterilise it, as per the instructions in the Bacon Jam introduction. You can also freeze it for up to 3 months. An ice cube tray works really well for individual portions.

METHOD

1. Fry the bacon in its own fat until it is golden brown. Pour the fried bacon and fat into a blender along with all of the other ingredients (it is best to add the other ingredients first. Blend until smooth and taste. If it is too thick for your taste add more vinegar, and if the honey becomes too sharp, add a little maple syrup to balance it. .

2. Decant into a sterilised bottle and store in the fridge for up to a week. You can freeze this sauce for up to 3 months (see above).

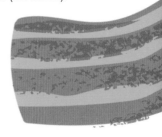

Bacon Curing

Bacon Curing

Curing bacon always seemed intimidating to me, before I understood how straightforward and easy it really is. Bacon is simply salt, sugar, and curing salt with time, and a little attention, but that is it.

There are many reasons why you should cure your own bacon. Chief among them are:

Tastier Bacon – It is not only easy to make your own bacon, you can get tastier results at home.

You can use better pork from sustainable farms – You can choose high-quality pork from sustainable sources, as opposed to pork from factory farms. Ethical concerns are really important, but there is also the simple fact that the better the meat is, the better the bacon is.

It is cheaper – Even when you use the best high-quality pork, your bacon at home will be cheaper than commercial bacon.

You can cure cuts that are hard to buy – Curing your own bacon allows you to make bacon that you just can't buy. You can cure lots of different cuts: chops, ribs, collar, just for starters.

You can get creative with flavour – You can add flavour. So much flavour. Once you have your 3 key ingredients: Curing Salt #1, Salt, and Sugar.

I have a lot of information on bacon curing, concerns about safety, and using nitrites in A Short Primer on Bacon Curing and Using Nitrites in the Small Baconpedia on p.229.

How to cure bacon at home

Now for the tasty fun stuff!

There are several ways of curing bacon. Initially, I wanted to provide a thorough, detailed look at all of these so that you could make your choices, and wrote what was tantamount to an entire book on that. In the end, I realised that this was going against the spirit of this book, which is all about encouragement and embracing things in the kitchen (and the fridge!) that seemed complex but are actually very accessible.

I am focused on the best and safest curing options for the curious home cook. Rather than over-whelm you with information, let's start by actually curing bacon and enjoying the process and results. This is my take on how my bacon cures can be applied safely in the home kitchen, and not how they might be applied in a commercial situation.

Here are the various methods of curing bacon.

Wet or brine curing

Curing in a prepared brine in a large container in the fridge. You can get a more even cure this way when you are starting out, but you will dilute the flavours of any added aromatics, and that is where the fun and flavour is. The bacon absorbs water this way and you get shrinkage when you cook it. It is a bulky curing method too, which is not great for regular kitchens and fridges.

Dry curing

Application of a dry cure to the external surface of your pork. There is no liquid involved, hence the name. You then store it in the fridge for as long as it takes (I will explain this in a bit), usually in a sealed bag, turning it every 2 days. Moisture is drawn out of the meat this way, and the end result is a firmer piece of bacon with a better, fuller flavour. This is my preferred method, cured in the equilibrium curing style.

Equilibrium curing

Equilibrium curing is a more modern approach to old-school techniques like saltbox curing. Saltbox curing uses an excess of salt and offers little precision or control over the end result. This risks under-curing or producing bacon that is too salty.

With equilibrium curing, you weigh the pork and make a precise cure for the exact weight of the pork. In this way you get a salt level that is exactly what you planned for, and you control the nitrite level in your pork too.

It is common to vacuum pack these equilibrium dry cures. It works well and prevents cross-contamination, so it is excellent from a food safety perspective. Biodegradable bags for vacuum-pack machines are available now also.

This obviously requires an investment and is something you may not want to do straight away. It is also common to store the curing bacon in a bag that can be sealed, like a ziplock, so that the liquid that forms as it is curing doesn't leak.

Using nitrites

I use nitrites to cure bacon at home. Here is why:

Food safety – Nitrites are important for food safety (preventing botulism).

Taste – Nitrites are the key to bacon flavour. Nitrites ripen the bacon as it cures, creating its signature flavour in the process. Salt-cured pork without nitrites tastes good but it tastes of salt-pork, not bacon.

Health considerations – Nitrites are used in very small and well-controlled quantities. In terms of risks versus benefits, not contracting botulism is a very important consideration and tips the scales for me immediately.

The amount of nitrites that should be used in curing have been studied at length, specified and are inspected in industry. I apply the same rules to my cures (but don't worry, I won't come to your house to inspect your bacon, although I am sure it will be very very good).

It is important to use a scale that can measure to 0.1g as the amount of Curing Salt #1 that you will use is very small. These scales are very compact, inexpensive and an essential tool for the home curer.

How long does it take to cure bacon?

How long it takes to cook bacon depends entirely on how thick your bacon is. A good rule of thumb is one day for each centimetre thickness plus two days. For streaky bacon the average is 7 days and for back bacon 10 days. Using an equilibrium cure you don't need to stress about over curing up to 25% of the curing time. Try not to let it go longer than that.

The cure will work faster through thinner cuts of meat like chops and ribs (the bones don't need to be considered in the thickness). Skinless pork is your best bet because, as a beginner, the skin can be a barrier to the cure. If you want to keep the skin on, apply 90% of the cure to the flesh and 10% to the skin. The cure will work its way through the flesh to the skin and cure more evenly.

Basic bacon cure

We are going to use an equilibrium dry cure, as indicated above. It is best to apply the cure with gloves for food hygiene purposes.

For simplicity, I prefer to cure pork that has the skin and bones removed, unless I am curing ribs. If the skin and bones are still attached, I remove them and save the bones in the freezer for broth and make crackling or chicharron with the skin. Trim the meat so that it is in a neat rectangle so that it cures evenly. You can use any offcuts in the kitchen.

I suggest you start with this simple straightforward cure that you can adapt as you feel more comfortable with the process, or you can use some of my suggested adaptations that follow. Measure the height of your pork and calculate the curing days according to the rule: cure in the fridge for one day for each centimetre thickness plus two days at the end, and turn every two days, taking care that all of the liquid remains in the bag and doesn't spill.

Weigh your pork and, using your precise scale, create a cure using the following measurements:

2.25% salt *(I use fine sea salt)*
0.25% curing salt #1/Prague Powder
1% sugar *(you can use any sugar, I prefer soft brown sugar or demerara)*

1. Apply the cure to the surface of the pork with clean, food-safe gloves, ensuring it is well distributed and every nook and cranny has cure on it.

It won't seem like a lot of cure, but it is enough and you shouldn't add any more. It will make its way through the meat as it cures.

2. Place the pork in a bag that you can seal. You can get reusable bags that seal, just make sure they are clean, or use ziplock bags (although personally I am trying to avoid single-use plastics).

3. Use the curing days calculation (see intro above) based on the height of your pork as a guide to number of curing days. When the bacon is ready it will be firm to the touch and pink the whole way through, with no soft spots.

Big-batch bacon curing with regular kitchen scales

If you don't have your scales yet, and want to get started, we have options. We can make a large batch of a simple curing mixture and then measure out larger amounts of that every time we cure bacon. We should still aim to be very accurate with this, so I would only recommend using this approach for larger amounts of meat.

I would always encourage you to invest in set of small accurate scales that measures to 0.1g as discussed already. Mine is so small it lives in my equally very small cutlery drawer and it cost £7 (USD $9). With this precision, I can cure one pork chop for myself.

In terms of proportions, I use 2.5% fine sea salt or kosher salt (if you like it saltier, you can go up to 3%), 0.25% curing salt #1 and 1% sugar. We have to cure a large amount to make sure the cure amounts are accurate for best results and for safety reasons.

Measure your pork also so that you can source a big sealable bag to accommodate this joint.

For 2kg (4½ lb) of pork:

Curing salt #1	5g
Fine sea salt or kosher salt	50g
Sugar	20g

Apply the basic cure ingredients as per the Basic Bacon Cure recipe. Follow the recipe to completion. Remember to rinse off the cure at the end.

You can add any of the other suggestions from the recipes preceding, just make sure you double them, as those recipes are for 1kg (2¼ lb) of pork, not the 2kg (4½ lb) pork curing suggested here.

Smoking home-cured bacon

Once your bacon is cured, you can leave it as it is, which is green bacon. Or you can smoke it. Smoking was traditionally used as a food preservation technique, and that is true here too, but we are mainly doing this for flavour.

Cold-smoking is the traditional way and you can purchase cold smokers for this process if you become a serious bacon curer. You can also make one from old filing cabinets, even a metal sieve.

Once your curing process is complete, rinse the cure off the meat. The cure will have penetrated right through the meat, we just want to get rid of any excess. Don't soak the bacon. You only soak bacon that has been cured with too much salt, whether this has been by choice or not. We used a precise equilibrium curing method so we know that the salt level will be just right.

The next step is to form a pellicle on your bacon. This is a skin that develops as the bacon air dries that keeps the bacon moist and gives the smoke something to cling on to. The easiest way to do this is to put the bacon on a wire rack on a tray in the fridge and leave it exposed to the dry air for 48 hours.

Here, I offer solutions for the home cook embarking on an adventure who doesn't yet have all the kit, and just wants to try it before committing to making room for a smoker in their life. There are so many clever solutions online and I encourage you to explore them.

Here are two home-smoking suggestions that I like.

Smoking your bacon on the BBQ

Set up your BBQ for indirect heat and smoke your bacon fat side up at 110°C/225°F over some soaked woodchips (the kind of wood is up to you!), until it reaches an internal temperature as measured by a thermometer of 66°C/150°F. It should take about 2 hours.

Smoking your bacon in the oven

1. Use a roasting pan with a rack that fits inside it for this. Line the pan with enough foil to cover the bottom of the pan and extend over the bacon with room inside for the smoke to circulate.

2. Preheat your oven to 95°C/75°C Fan (200°F).

3. Soak enough woodchips to just cover the bottom of a pan. Once you've drained the woodchips, line the bottom of your pan with foil and scatter the woodchips on it. Put an oven rack over the woodchips and place the bacon fat side-up on the rack. Now carefully seal the foil around the bacon without actually touching it, allowing lots of room for the smoke to circulate.

4. Allow the bacon to smoke until the internal temperature, as checked by thermometer, reaches 66°C/150°F. This will takeabout 2 hours also, maybe up to 2.5 hours.

Favourite creative bacon cures from my kitchen

I whittled down my very long recipe-curing list to the ones that I share here, which are my favourite flavours, and excellent starting points for you on your personal bacon-curing journey. The following recipes assume 1kg (2¼ lb) of pork. Divide or multiply accordingly for your bacon recipe.

Maple bacon

Sweet-cured bacon is a real treat. You can use your favourite sugar, and here I am using one of mine: maple syrup!

1. Follow the instructions for Basic Bacon Cure and after you have already applied the dry cure to the pork add 100ml (3½ fl oz) maple syrup directly to the bag per kilo of pork. Seal the bag and gently rotate to ensure liquid is well distributed.

2. Carry on with the rest of the Basic Bacon Cure recipe remembering to rinse off the cure at the end..

Hot toddy bacon

1. Combine 100ml (4fl oz) of good whiskey and 50ml (2fl oz) honey and stir well.

2. Follow the instructions for Basic Bacon Cure and add the prepared liquid direct to the bag after you have already applied the dry cure to the pork.

3. Seal the bag and gently rotate it to ensure liquid is well distributed. Carry on with the rest of the Basic Bacon Cure recipe. Remember to rinse off the cure at the end..

Miso maple bacon

1. Follow the instructions for Basic Bacon Cure and before putting it in the bag, pat 50g (1¼ oz) of white miso gently on top of the cure all over the pork and place in the bag.

2. Add 25ml (1fl oz) of maple syrup directly to the bag, seal it and rotate it gently to evenly distribute the maple syrup. Carry on with the rest of the Basic Bacon Cure recipe. Remember to rinse off the cure at the end..

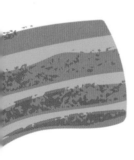

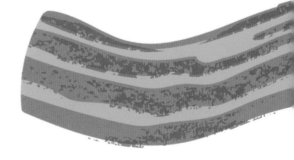

Stout and treacle bacon

1. Heat 100ml (3½ fl oz) stout and 25g (1 oz) treacle until the treacle has just dissolved and cool completely.

2. Follow the instructions for Basic Bacon Cure and add the liquid to the bag once the pork with cure has already been added. Seal it and rotate it gently to evenly distribute the stout and treacle. Carry on with the rest of the Basic Bacon Cure recipe. Remember to rinse off the cure at the end..

Seaweed bacon

I adore seaweed, its intense umami and brilliant flavours make for an excellent bacon cure. I use dried dulse, which is a favourite.

1. Grind 10g (¼ oz) of dried dulse and 5 black peppercorns to a powder in a blender or a spice grinder. It is easier to do this if you cut the dulse really small first.

2. Apply the basic cure ingredients as per the Basic Bacon Cure recipe. Follow by patting the dulse-pepper mix all over the flesh. Follow the recipe to completion. Remember to rinse off the cure at the end.

Gochujang, soy and lime bacon

I adore gochujang (Korean fermented pepper paste). It is not its first appearance in this book and it makes a great addition to a bacon cure.

1. Whisk 50g (2 oz) of gochujang paste, 50ml (2 fl oz) soy sauce or tamari and the juice of one lime until well combined.

2. Follow the instructions for Basic Bacon Cure and add the liquid to the bag once the pork with cure has already been added. Seal it and rotate it gently to evenly distribute the stout and treacle. Carry on with the rest of the Basic Bacon Cure recipe. Remember to rinse off the cure at the end.

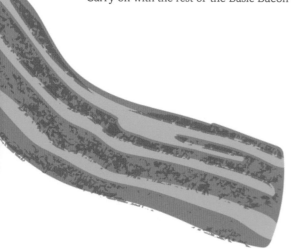

Small Baconpedia

Curing bacon in the traditional Irish way

BACON

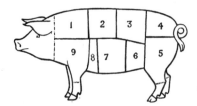

1. Collar.
2. Back and Ribs.
3. Long Loin.
4. Corner Gammon ⎰ Gammon or
5. Gammon Hock ⎱ Ham.

6. Flank.
7. Thin Streaky.
8. Thick Streaky.
9. Shoulder or Fore Hock.
10. Head.

METHODS OF COOKING

Collar : may be boiled, or sliced and fried.

Back
Long Loin ⎱ Expensive part. Usually cut for rashers.

Corner Gammon
Gammon Hock ⎱ May be boiled or baked, sometimes boned.

Flank : Economical part—used for boiling.

Thin Streaky : May be cut for rashers, or used for boiling.

Thick Streaky : Cut for rashers or used for boiling.

Shoulder : Used for boiling, sometimes boned.

Porksteak : Removed from the loin before curing, and sold fresh.

Head : Used for boiling.

This brilliant page from seminal Irish cookbook and school textbook "All in the Cooking, Coláiste Mhuire Book of Advanced Cookery" (by Josephine B. Marnell, Nora M. Breathnach, Ann A. Martin and Mor Murnaghan) illustrates how key bacon was and is in Irish food culture.

The whole pig can be cured, and often was. This is why bacon in Ireland is so much more than rashers. "All in the Cooking" was first published in 1946 and was widely used in education until the 1970s.

I have two copies. One was my mother's school book, which my grandmother used right up until she died, aged 90. It was also reprinted by The O'Brien Press Ltd. and The Educational Company of Ireland and I bought one of those copies also. You can too! It is available to purchase online.

Reproduced with kind permission from "All in the Cooking, Coláiste Mhuire Book of Advanced Cookery" (by Josephine B. Marnell, Nora M. Breathnach, Ann A. Martin and Mor Murnaghan) by The O'Brien Press Ltd. and The Educational Company of Ireland.

A short primer on bacon curing and using nitrites

If you are in any way interested in bacon (and hello, there you are, so you must be!), it is likely that you are curious about the details around curing your own, the use of nitrites and any health impacts.

Point to note: when I reference salt here, I mean table salts such as sea salt, kosher salt etc.

Why do we use nitrites in bacon curing?

Humans have been curing meats for thousands of years. Originally with table salt and smoke, but nitrites and nitrates were being used by the Ancient Greeks and Romans, who used saltpetre (which is potassium nitrate) with citrus to cure and preserve meats.

The combination of salt and saltpetre in meat curing has been common since medieval times. We still use it today. We now know that saltpetre is effective because of the nitrites formed by the reduction of nitrates as the meat cures.

With this knowledge, curing salts for bacon and other quick-cure meats to be cooked were developed. These contain nitrites and act faster, because we don't need to wait for the nitrates to be converted to nitrites. We are good to go.

For bacon, we use Curing Salt #1, also called Prague Powder or "pink salt" which is a combination of table salt (93.75%) and sodium nitrite (6.25%).

Nitrites are used in the bacon curing process for three main reasons:

-       Food safety - nitrites inhibit the growth of bacteria like Clostridium botulinum which can thrive in meat curing conditions. It is extremely effective. So, the use of nitrites helps prevent botulism that can come from bacteria thriving in these conditions. Side note: the word botulism comes from the German for sausage poisoning.

-       Nitrites are involved in ripening the meat as it cures and are key to the flavour.

-       Nitrites are the reason why bacon is pink.

So, if you cure pork without nitrites, the end product won't be pink and it won't taste the same. It won't be what we know as bacon.

It is easy to be scared of nitrites because we don't hear their name often but it is important to remember that they exist naturally in foods such as leafy greens, celery, and beetroot, in high quantities. In Europe, analysis of dietary sources of nitrites indicated that 80% comes from vegetables and 5% comes from cured meats.

We use tiny amounts of sodium nitrite when we cure bacon. The quantities of nitrite used in bacon and cured meats are very tightly controlled by law. It is important that we apply the same concerns and controls when we make bacon at home.

So, those recipes that say 1 tsp of curing or pink salt? Don't use those. You could very easily add an excess of nitrites which could be harmful. Nitrites in bacon are very carefully controlled because in larger amounts they are extremely toxic. Or you may undercure your meat which wouldn't be safe.

It is as important to be precise at home with bacon curing as it is in a commercial facility. It is really easy too. You just need to be precise to 0.1g with Curing Salt #1 as you use such tiny amounts when making bacon. How? It is just a matter of having precise scales, and they are easy to source, compact and relatively inexpensive (mine was £7).

What about the health risks?

The issue with nitrites in cured meats such as bacon is that they form nitrosamines while cooking in very hot pans, and while digesting. These nitrosamines have been linked to cancer.

I spent a lot of time reading EU documents on food additives and cured meats, scientific research on nitrites in food and their impact on health, including their potential carcinogenic activity. I also read the WHO research on this issue, so you wouldn't have to. Someone give me a medal! (Do, please).

What are the issues with nitrites in bacon?

Before I launch into this, I want to express that I have huge admiration and respect for the WHO and science generally.

I started out in science, studying it at university and then pursuing a career in scientific publishing at one of the world's oldest and foremost science magazines. My passion for food and writing drew me out of there eventually, and here I am.

According to a WHO study in 2015: "An analysis of data from 10 studies estimated that every 50 gram portion of processed meat eaten daily increases the risk of colorectal cancer by about 18%". The study did not evaluate comparisons with people who have vegetarian and vegan diets, or ingestion of poultry or fish, nor did it look at other lifestyle aspects of the people affected that may determine other causes of cancer.

So this investigation - which was an analysis of many existing studies - saw a causal link that we should know about. What it says is that people who eat cured meats every day are 18% more likely to get colorectal cancer. It doesn't take into account other lifestyle factors that may affect the observed link.

There clearly is an issue that we need to be aware of, and we absolutely need to take this into consideration.

What about nitrite-free bacon? Can't we do that?

Yes, there is bacon labelled "nitrite-free" in the shops. What isn't clear with these is that this bacon has actually been cured with nitrites. It is just that those nitrites came from natural sources, for example celery. Nitrites from celery are the same as nitrites from anywhere else. Our body doesn't distinguish between them.

It would be more accurate to say that these bacons are "Synthetic Sodium Nitrite Free or Artificial Preservative Free". It is important to say that not all additives are bad, this is a misconception, and a chemical created in a lab is the same as the same chemical in nature (in this case nitrite is NO2). Additives don't always equal heavily processed food.

The problem with using celery powder or similar to cure your bacon at home is that you have no idea how many nitrites are in there. There could be a lot, there may not be enough. It is much safer and easier to use a precise curing salt developed for the purpose with scales accurate to 0.1g.

Making nitrite-free bacon without any artificial or natural sources of nitrite, such as celery, results in a salted pork that just doesn't taste like bacon. It usually has an unappetizing brown colour too.

My conclusion

This is my own conclusion. It is not a recommendation, I am not a doctor or a scientist (anymore!). My aim is to present the evidence to you clearly and try to answer any questions that you might have.

I am not going to pretend that bacon is a health food, but it is also very important that we don't fear our food and that we are rational in response to perceived risks. There was a time when we thought that butter and fat were bad for us and were to be avoided and at least reduced. This was proved to be incorrect. Fats are essential in a healthy balanced diet. The same goes for eggs. Sugar is an issue, and we know this, yet we still enjoy sugar in moderation.

It is a frequent misinterpretation that people who enjoy meat reject any fruit and vegetables. I eat meat and fish, and I also aim to have 7 portions of fruit and veg every day, as is recommended for a healthy diet. Many of my meals have no meat or fish in them at all. Balance in all things is so important. Even the most ardent meat eater is not a carnivore but an omnivore.

The most important thing in a healthy diet is to avoid ultra processed food which has low nutritional value and has been linked to higher rates of cardiovascular disease and death (British Medical Journal, May 2019). A healthier lifestyle involves making as much of your own food as you can with fresh ingredients, where possible.

When you have a healthy balanced diet, you can indulge in treats every now and then. We all know cake is not necessarily a healthy choice, the same goes for Candied Bacon Fudge. But how good are they?! So good! A balm for the soul on occasion.

I love cooking bacon, and, of course, eating it. I believe that we can enjoy bacon and cured meats occasionally, even though we shouldn't eat them every day. I care about my health, and I also care about yours. If I thought that bacon presented a serious health hazard, I would never have published this book.

Bacon and cured meats can be a small part of an otherwise balanced healthy diet. With this book, I want bacon lovers to enjoy all of the possibilities, to cook different things, and to find pleasure in the kitchen and at the table. Especially on hard days. The kitchen is where I find solace and nourishment, and not just for the belly.

If you are ready to get started, you can get Curing Salt #1 from bacon and sausage curing shops online (there are many!) and source a precision digital scale. Head to the Bacon Curing chapter on P216 for details on the process, details on curing bacon at home safely, and recipes.

Your Bacon Space

I started this book, now you get to finish it with recipes and notes of your own. I always wished there were notes pages in favourite cookbooks so that I could add my scribbles.

Every cookbook starts with the writer, but the minute it lands in your hands, it is yours. A cookbook for me is a starting point, a journey to somewhere delicious and fun, often an education, especially when it is an immersion in another cooking culture.

My hope is that with Bacon the Cookbook you don't just get a Big Bacon Energy (I couldn't resist) but also a Very Big Cooking Energy; that the little twists and turns you take with me on each recipe page, and the techniques that you pick up along the way, will inspire you to create your own inventions (and if you do, please let me know!).

I will continue to share new bacon recipes via baconthecookbook.com (and on the respective social media channels: @baconthecookbook on Instagram and Facebook) that you can add in these pages too. There is a newsletter on baconthecookbook.com that you can sign up for. It is infrequent but always worth it when it lands. Your data is safe with me and I won't spam you either.

There are two types of pages in this section: half for recipes, and arranged so that there's space for ingredients, notes and method. The other pages are for your bacon-inspired scribbles, your very own bacon scratchings with your pen.

Enjoy and thanks for joining me on this bacon journey! I hope you have as much fun with it as I did.

My Recipes

INGREDIENTS

NOTES

METHOD

My Recipes

INGREDIENTS

NOTES

METHOD

My Recipes

INGREDIENTS

NOTES

METHOD

My Recipes

INGREDIENTS

NOTES

METHOD

My Recipes

INGREDIENTS

NOTES

METHOD

My Recipes

INGREDIENTS

NOTES

METHOD

Notes

Notes

Notes

Notes

Notes

Notes

Notes

Notes

Notes

Notes

Bacon: The Cookbook Index

Acknowledgements

Firstly, I want to express an enormous thank you to everyone who backed this book. I am so very grateful for your support and encouragement. It gifted me an opportunity to create something that I could be fully immersed in and to remember why I do what I do, and how much I love it.

I am so very grateful for my incredibly talented team who helped this novice publisher/author/book distributor/forklift arranger, who wildly underestimated just how much she was taking on. They were all absolute superstars and a joy to work with.

To Tim Biddle for that wonderful cover art, layout design and illustration and being an absolute dream to work with.

To Karyn Noble for her expert, patient, careful and rigorous editing. Also a dream to work with!

Tim & Karyn deserve special mention for being there through the very intense final stages, and never blinking an eye.

To Georgia Glynn Smith for photography and a super-fun atmosphere to create in. It was wonderful, and I knew I had to work with Georgia again after she absolutely captured the energy of what I was doing with my first cookbook, Comfort & Spice. Georgia did the same here.

To Anita Mangan for art direction for photography; beautiful piggy and bacon illustrations used as backgrounds in some of the photography; provider of most of the tiny pigs; lots of laughs and initial page designs.

To Lara Brotherton and Siobhán Nagle for their very welcome helping hands and heads at the photoshoot.

To the people in my life who lived through this and deserve at least an award. Let's make them and call them the piggies. I am very grateful. You know who you are and you were absolute superstars, respecting when I couldn't and wouldn't talk about it and allowing me to talk about it at length otherwise.

Particular enormous thanks to Art, for living through this, and for being so patient and encouraging through all of it. It wasn't easy I know.

Thank YOU for buying the book. I hope you love this book as much as we loved making it.

Bacon the world a better place, one enthusiastic recipe at a time!

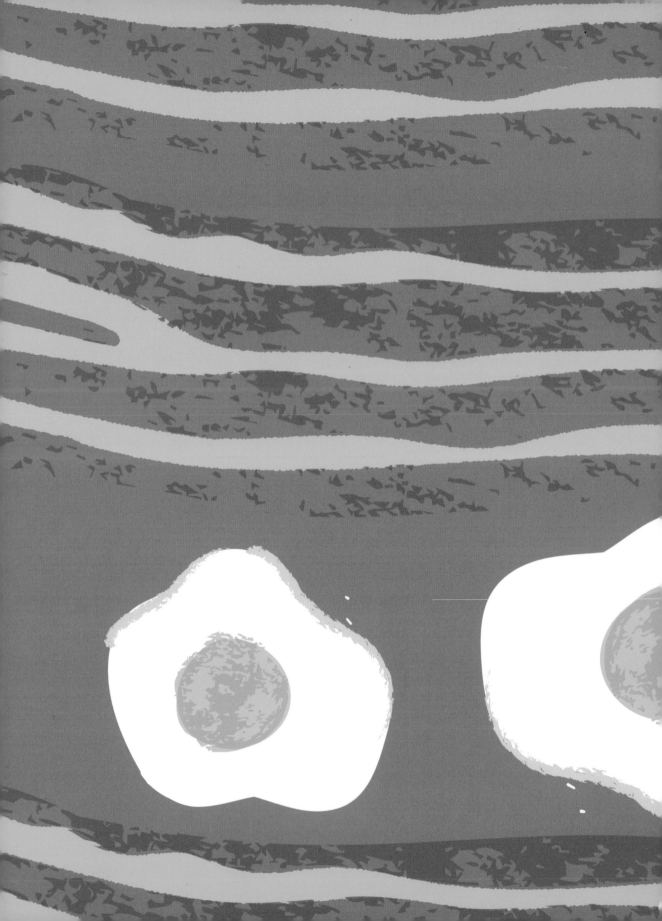